A Passion for Teaching

™

Association for Supervision and Curriculum Development
1703 N. Beauregard St. • Alexandria, VA 22311-1714 USA
Telephone: 1-800-933-2723 or 703-578-9600 • Fax: 703-575-5400
Web site: http://www.ascd.org • E-mail: member@ascd.org

Gene R. Carter, *Executive Director*

Michelle Terry, *Associate Executive Director, Program Development*

Nancy Modrak, *Director, Publishing*

John O'Neil, *Director of Acquisitions*

Julie Houtz, *Managing Editor of Books*

Darcie Simpson, *Associate Editor*

René Bahrenfuss, *Copy Editor*

Charles D. Halverson, *Project Assistant*

Gary Bloom, *Director, Design and Production Services*

Karen Monaco, *Senior Graphic Designer*

Tracey A. Smith, *Production Manager*

Dina Murray, *Production Coordinator*

John Franklin, *Production Coordinator*

Printed in the United States of America.

May 1999 member book (p). ASCD Premium, Comprehensive, and Regular members periodically receive ASCD books as part of their membership benefits. No. FY99-7.

ASCD Stock No. 199224

ASCD member price: $19.95   nonmember price: $23.95

Library of Congress Cataloging-in-Publication Data

A passion for teaching / conceived and edited by Sarah L. Levine
in collaboration with Scott McVay ; photographs by Kit Frost.
    p. cm.
    Includes bibliographical references (p.).
    ISBN 0-87120-354-5 (alk. paper)
    1. Teachers—United States Anecdotes. 2. Teaching—United States
Anecdotes. I. Levine, Sarah L. (Sarah Loewenberg), 1946-
II. McVay, Scott.
    LB1775.2 .P37 1999
    371.1—dc21
                                        99-6340
                                        CIP
                                        Rev.

04 03 02 01 00 99   10 9 8 7 6 5 4 3 2 1

A Passion
FOR TEACHING

Conceived and Edited by SARAH L. LEVINE

in collaboration with SCOTT MCVAY

Photographs by KIT FROST

Association for Supervision and Curriculum Development
Alexandria, Virginia USA

A Passion for Teaching

The Power of Words

Reflections

Teacher/Mentors

After Words

Sarah L. Levine
School Head, Teacher, Teacher of Teachers
Polytechnic School
Pasadena, California
30 years

A Celebration of Teachers and Teaching

Sarah L. Levine

THIS BOOK CELEBRATES TEACHERS AND teaching. It contains the artistry and wisdom of 42 teachers who have remained passionate about classroom teaching for many years. Their words and their work describe the deep connections they have forged with students and with the profession. They identify some of the reasons teachers can sustain their vitality in the classroom; they make palpable the enormous influence of impassioned teaching and learning.

I am always amazed that teachers are not more widely prized for their complex, demanding, and essential work. Generalizations about teachers and teaching do not reflect the quality and dedication of the vast majority of women and men who work in schools. In particular, negative characterizations of teachers at the middle and later stages of their careers belie the continuing desire of adults to grow and learn. They minimize the many unique opportunities teachers have to interact with and influence the students they teach. Most significantly, these characterizations diminish the vital importance of teaching and learning.

The seeds for this project were sown long ago. As a teacher of children and adults for 30 years, I have a deep, personal passion for teaching. I worked at the Harvard Graduate School of Education over a period of 15 years as a graduate student and then as Associate Director of the Harvard Principals' Center and Lecturer on Education. In these roles, I was immersed first in my own writing and then in encouraging practitioners to reflect on and write about their work. As head of two schools (Belmont Day School, Belmont, Massachusetts, and Polytechnic School, Pasadena, California), I have witnessed firsthand the incredible energy and dedication of senior teachers.

My interest in schools as contexts for adult growth led to my involvement with a two-year project focused on the professional development of experienced teachers. A grant from the Edward E. Ford Foundation through the Association of Independent Schools of New England allowed me and several other school leaders to bring together teachers with 15 or more years of classroom teaching who continued to be excited by teaching. In the first year, teacher/participants were selected by their school heads; in year two, these teachers were joined by others who became aware of the opportunity and applied to take part. By the end of the second year, some 150 teachers had shared stories, initiated projects, designed and taken part in professional development activities, and made presentations about key educational issues.

I was not at all surprised by the energy and wisdom of these senior teachers. I was immediately struck, however, by the rare opportunity of capturing and sharing their energy with others. Since I had worked with both public and private school teachers during my time at Harvard, I knew that senior teachers in all types of schools had something valuable to share. Having recently worked with the Geraldine R. Dodge Foundation on another school-based project, I was aware of the Foundation's long and distinguished history with schools.

When I phoned Dodge Foundation Executive Director Scott McVay with the idea for the project, I was not at all surprised by his enthusiasm. He talked immediately about the experienced public school teachers in New Jersey that the Foundation has worked with in a wide range of projects. Wouldn't it be fun to see, he and I mused, how the experiences of the teachers we were each working with from independent and public school settings would compare by inviting them to write about their sustained interest in teaching? Could we learn what keeps teachers alive to teaching over time from asking them to reflect on their years in the classroom?

Several months later, my proposal to the Foundation was approved, and the project was off and running. To gather the first 10 entries, we invited the teachers we were each currently working with to send submissions. "What about expanding our vision beyond the collection of short essays?" I wondered out loud to Scott. How about seeking a range of submissions: short essays, poems, drawings, short stories, cartoons, and photographs? From more than 80 initial entries, we selected the work of 11 teachers in the first round, including several essays, a short story, a short play, poems, drawings, and paintings.

We then went national and international with our search for passionate teachers, advertising in educational journals. These included *NEA Today, Educational Leadership, Independent School Journal,* and *Education Week.* Some publishers were so interested in the idea they provided free advertising. In addition, editors from regional organizations saw the call for papers and agreed to run ads in their newsletters and other publications.

More than 200 teachers from around the United States and abroad responded to a "call for papers and/or artwork" for the project: *What ideas and experiences have kept you vital and alive to teaching and learning?* In addition to the wide range of materials they submitted, many took time to write about how much it meant to see the work of teachers recognized, independent of whether their contribution was chosen. The project design included creating a review committee composed of the teachers whose submissions Scott and I initially selected. After the review process, they commented:

• "Reading the submissions has been both exhilarating and humbling, far more than I can express. I am renewed by the incredible spirit, creativity, and love expressed in these offerings."

• "I found myself reflecting on [many of these pieces] as I prepared my lessons in the days following their reading. I found myself sharing with friends, colleagues, and family members. [These are the pieces] that will remain with me always, whether or not they are published."

• "Some of the entries brought me to tears."

In fact, Scott and I were frequently moved by the power of the entries. Scott was so taken by the booklet created by Lucienne Bond Simon and her 2nd graders to save the arts in the Louisiana public schools that he called her directly and ordered 100 copies. Sometimes in our conversations, we read things out loud to demonstrate our emotional responses. When an essay, poem, photograph, or drawing came in, I was often so moved that I shared it with friends and colleagues. As you will soon experience, many bring nods of recognition, some bring smiles, and others elicit tears.

The idea of including photographs with each selection emerged from my sense that seeing the authors in the context created by their work would add depth and dimension. Once again, Scott and the Foundation responded quickly and favorably. Kit Frost, herself a senior teacher, had moved from New Jersey to Colorado, where she is developing a community arts studio for youth and adults. Familiar with both her teaching and her photography, Scott thought she would be just the right person to include on the project. Over more than a year, Kit read the selected pieces, traveled to the schools of the authors/artists/teachers, and captured images that complement their work. Each photograph is accompanied by information about the senior teacher at the time of his or her submission.

The words and images of the teachers you will come to know in this book crystallize some of its most salient messages. Senior teacher Lois Marie Harrod's poem, "This Is a Story You Already Know," describes the particular story of one of her high school students. It also points out a poignant irony about teachers and teaching. All of us have gone to school; few of us acknowledge the influence of our school experience. "It's All About Remembering," explains Suzanne Snyder-Carroll, looking back on her own school days after 20 years of teaching at Hopewell Valley Central High School in Pennington, New Jersey. It's all about "The Call to Teach" says Vickie Gill, an 18-year veteran teacher of English, reading, and journalism from Tennessee. It's about "The First Day of School" writes Richard A. Lawson—even after 21 first days with 3rd and 4th graders at Nueva School in Hillsborough, California.

Like Hamilton Salsich, middle school teacher at Pine Point School in Stonington, Connecticut, and a 25 year veteran, the teachers in this book are all "Living Well in the Classroom." "What Could Be Better?" asks Justine Heinrichs, String and Orchestra Director for 6th through 12th grades at Holland Hall School in Tulsa, Oklahoma. She goes on to enumerate the lessons she has taught her students over 15 years—beyond learning to play a musical instrument. Carter Jason Sio's reflections on 15 years with the woodworking and design program at George School in Pennsylvania— "Shop Thoughts"—capture a piece of what this book offers: comments and conversation about sustained teaching and learning.

Whether our memories of school are good or bad, we are all likely to recognize many of the experiences and ideas expressed in this book. Maybe we learned something in school that changed our view of the world. Perhaps we made a powerful connection to another person during our school years. Quite possibly we had a teacher who made an indelible imprint upon our life. To what other institution or to what other enterprise can so many attribute such life-altering influences?

I have many hopes for this publication. I hope that teachers at every point in their careers will feel celebrated and elevated by the contributions of these senior teachers. I hope that people outside the profession will have a new or renewed faith in teachers, a reverence for teaching. I hope that some who have not previously considered "a call to teach" will recognize both the demands and rewards and consider the profession.

The vision for this book has some rewarding applications. I challenge schools and professional organizations to collect and share the work of teachers among their constituencies. The benefits can be both immediate and lasting. Teachers at all stages of their careers will gain from reflecting on, articulating, and showcasing their work; readers will gain an appreciation for the talents and expertise of teachers; teachers and readers will gain a renewed sense of the value and joy of the profession.

Wei-ling Wu teaches Chinese at West Windsor-Plainsboro High School in Princeton Junction, New Jersey. Her reflections on the value of teaching draw from the ancient Chinese master teacher, Confucius. His words express an essential truth for the vital senior teacher:

> When one is very determined,
> One forgets about eating;
> When one is very happy,
> One forgets about being sad;
> When one is very determined and very happy,
> One forgets about getting old.

Wei-ling Wu's own words capture a truth for herself and for teachers everywhere: "We have boundless joy and tremendous passion for being teachers."

Working on this project with Scott McVay, Kit Frost, and the teachers who graciously share themselves for the benefit of others has been a privilege. As the title of Kit's reflections states, these teachers have given us the "honor to witness" what happens inside the lives of teachers and children when we take the time to open the classroom door.

Acknowledgments

THIS PROJECT REFLECTS THE WORK of many. I'd like to thank the hundreds of senior teachers who submitted their work for consideration. In addition to taking the time to reflect on their long-time commitment to the profession, each of these teachers has sustained an interest in and love for teaching. Thank you to the teachers whose work is part of the book. Ten teachers participated in the review and selection of subsequent contributions. Special thanks to David Downing for his editorial suggestions.

I am grateful to the Geraldine R. Dodge Foundation for all of the support the Foundation gives to education and for the initial funding of this project. Executive Director Scott McVay immediately saw the value of the book and has been a magnificent collaborator. Thanks also to his staff and, most particularly, to Susan Pilshaw and Vera Dumont.

Koreen McQuilton served as my administrative assistant during the formative stages of the project. Koreen tracked correspondence, entered data, reviewed entries, and kept mounds of material organized.

Kit Frost is herself a veteran teacher. Currently working as a professional photographer in Durango, Colorado, she eagerly joined the project once the contributing teachers had been selected. With camera in hand, she traveled to each senior teacher's school, capturing them on film and thereby creating a visual complement to their words and their work. She contributed substantially to the design and layout of the book.

Finally, I am grateful to ASCD, especially to Nancy Modrak, John O'Neil, Julie Houtz, and Darcie Simpson for their enthusiastic response to the project and their excellent work on the book.

—*Sarah L. Levine*

Beginnings

Richard A. Lawson
3rd and 4th Grade Teacher
Nueva School
Hillsborough, California
21 years

The First Day of School

Richard A. Lawson

and what are the important questions anyway
on this first day of school after a night of no sleep
wondering even fearing how this day will go and all the rest
hoping it unfolds neatly as lesson plans promise
probably not and in that thought works a hint of unreadiness
and a quiet panic that hovers through the black coffee
yet later when we gather in first morning expectancy
we do manage to breathe though not deeply
my years are useless I am as new here
when the bell rings as all of those now looking at me

but what is this day and all the rest about
not of course rules and study habits or even
a bag full of knowledge somehow packed
in all those books tidy on each desk
rather an urge to know that pushes us into
wondering about clouds becoming raindrops
from another side of the world or why the flower
outside the window blooms at this precise moment
where the songs in my heart come from
and where are they going all those questions not in my curriculum
guide but that I now see in a new girl who can't stay
in her seat and dances an interruption around the room
negotiates attention in midsentence and at the end of my wits
tells me a story during lunch that is dazzling and profound
and in one brief moment I see her soul in love with imagination
that must move and wave and try to fly
and this is what I must relearn on this first day

that in our remembered self is an urge to create
I can look for it or not but my choice had better
be made with love and reverence for what we all want to express
our unique genius no matter what because that is
who we are and after all the only question
worth considering anyway no wonder the night
is full of sleeplessness this is a question of life
nothing else comes close I remember now why
I'm here and frightened
and so in awe of this moment
and these children

Bettye T. Spinner
12th Grade English Teacher
Moorestown High School
Moorestown, New Jersey
30 years

Sustaining the Wonder of Teaching

Bettye T. Spinner

"LITTLE MISS MUFFET SAT ON A tuffet . . . ." It was the first week of 1st grade. Miss Avery's voice floated toward me, as hypnotic as the sway of a pocket watch dangled from a magician's hand, so mesmerizing that I was no longer that shy little girl who had been prodded into taking the chair at the front of the class. I was no longer "acting out" the nursery rhyme. I had become Miss Muffet.

The wooden stool was a soft cushion beneath me as I delighted in each delicious mouthful of curds and whey (knowing neither taste nor appearance—or even the existence—of that strange food). At the sight of an imaginary spider, I bounded to my feet, and my shriek was echoed by my classmates who suddenly, too, saw arachnids beside them! When Miss Avery had restored us to embarrassed calm, she laughingly named me "actress of the day" and presented me with an impromptu Academy Award, an apple from her lunch bag.

Years later, I realized that my first official schoolteacher (at the time there was no public kindergarten for African Americans in my hometown) had given me an infinitely more precious gift than fruit. She had offered me food for a lifetime for, magically, she had stirred my imagination beyond anything I had known before. She had led me to create a reality that transcended the present moment. I knew, at 6, that one day I would become a teacher.

Not that my recognition of the power of school was new. Years before we reached high school and the study of Alexander Pope, children in my family all knew well that "a little learning is a dangerous thing." The youngest inevitably mastered that wisdom when accepted as a player in "school," the favorite family game. At 5, I was honored to be included, despite my infamous role—with its stool, pointed paper hat, and the rap of a ruler on my knuckles for each wrong answer. As if by magic, my right answers increased. Stroked into blossoming awareness of the power of knowledge to change the human condition, I wanted desperately to know everything my brother and sisters held in their encyclopedic minds.

Both school experiences resulted in magical discovery, but by what different means! My sibling teachers motivated by intimidation, by a fear of the consequences of being wrong. Miss Avery, on the other hand, motivated by creative questing, shepherding our timid steps over unfamiliar fertile ground. Long before *response theory* and *cooperative learning* resounded in the language of education, long before I had read Adrienne Rich's work, *When We Dead Awaken*, I knew I wanted what Miss Avery had: the kind of transforming magic that enables students to "re-vision" themselves and thus create their own knowing. Gently demanding, she demonstrated clearly that teaching is artful revelation.

My own career as a teacher of English, speech, and drama began at the Cleveland high school from which, the principal announced proudly during my interview, Jesse Owens had graduated. On late evenings that fall, as I locked my classroom and walked the silent halls to the exit, I often imagined the Olympic track star as a student there. I wondered how many of my students held his image for themselves. When I asked them, they lowered their eyes, as if embarrassed. But they smiled and applauded when I told them, "I'm no athlete, just an English teacher, but work with me and perhaps we can make you an 'Owens of the Mind.'" November weeks began to pass as quickly as weekends and, when I began to be impatient for the arrival of Mondays, I knew without question I was where I belonged: in the classroom, facilitating the magic of learning.

I taught in Cleveland for just a year, sadly aware that I would have to change schools frequently. Following my new husband wherever his military career led him was a bittersweet fate. I moved swiftly to classrooms in New York, the District of Columbia, France, Washington, Maryland, Germany, and Virginia. Obviously, the bitterness of my fate arose from the constant leaving of students, colleagues, and places I treasured. The sweetness, however, was in the arriving, in the challenges to my certainty that within each new cluster of infinite differences nestled the creative familiar. The magic was always there, on occasion deeply buried but awaiting discovery, if I could find my path to it.

When finally my life settled in one New Jersey town and one school, I realized what crucial incentive those frequent moves had given me to reassess and revitalize my role as a teacher. I realized, too, how easily *stability* can become *stasis*, a stubborn reliance upon the known and resistance to change. It became clear to me that vital teaching requires constant involvement in learning, a teacher/learner reciprocity, each role creating re-visions of the other. There followed then a sabbatical year to study and write, seven summers as a scholar in seminars and institutes of the National Endowment of the Humanities, critical participation in programs of the National Council of Teachers of English and our state affiliate, serving as a teacher advisor and poet with the Geraldine R. Dodge Foundation, and leading diversity workshops for the National SEED Project on Inclusive Curriculum.

Perhaps all of these experiences derived solely from my personal need for survival of the mind. The English teacher in me, however, savors the hope that words are keys to understanding, that something I learn in open exchange among my peers may prompt, even if momentarily and for a single student, the discovery or recovery of that wonder I found in my first encounter with learning. What could be better!

Harvest Home

Bettye T. Spinner

In the ideal
it is a harvesting,
this work we do—
a reaping of crops grown
from ancestral seeds,
a gathering of first fruit
from vines that trace their sources
 beyond geography,
 beyond gender,
 beyond the bleach
  and blush
   and black of skin
and root themselves in watery grace,
in knowledge that nurtures us all.

In the ideal
our classrooms fill, like cornucopia,
overflowing with the bounty of our grange.
Life stories, heaped among the texts,
spill into hallways of our schools,
crowd the sidewalks or the subways
or ride yellow buses home,
altering the form of knowing,
changing heads,
 changing hearts,
  changing history,
bringing harvest
home.

Victoria M. Gill
9th–12th Grade English, Reading, and Journalism Teacher
Cheatham County High School
Ashland City, Tennessee
18 years

The Call to Teach

Victoria M. Gill

I BECAME A TEACHER BECAUSE I detested school—hated just about every minute of it, particularly from 6th grade on. By the time I was in 8th grade I had a chair of my own right outside the vice-principal's office. I was a teacher's nightmare—the one in the back of the class making noises and comments to make the kids around me laugh. I constantly asked the dreaded question, "Why do we have to learn this junk, anyway?" My teachers would warn me not to get smart with them, which had always struck me as a contradiction in terms. I would read every book on the suggested reading lists sent home by my English teachers, but I refused to admit that I'd read the books. I didn't want to give them the satisfaction of thinking that they had taught me something. I hiked my skirts up, ratted my hair, and sported heavy black eyeliner and white lipstick. When the vice-principal would pull me into her office to wash my face, unroll my skirts, and comb out my hair, I'd march to the closest restroom and redo the whole thing. I was one of the girls who wouldn't let anyone else into the bathrooms at lunch because my friends and I were in there smoking.

In my junior year of high school, my counselor called me in to "discuss my future," one of his minimum job requirements. This man had never taken any notice of me before other than to make big circles around my chair outside the vice-principal's door. He sat me in his office, winced as he perused my rather thick disciplinary file, sighed, and asked me what I planned to do when I grew up. I smiled and told him I was going to be a teacher. He laughed, looked me dead in the eye, and said, "You'll never be a teacher." I got up, leaned over his desk and said, "You don't know me," and walked out of his office.

I knew I was going to be a teacher since I was 5 years old: It was the only thing I'd ever wanted to do. Even when I was acting out in school, causing a couple of teachers to reconsider their chosen profession, I knew teaching was one of the reasons I was put on this earth. I believe my attitude toward school would have been very different if I'd had even one teacher try to figure out why I was acting like such a jerk. I knew there had to be a better way, so I built my teaching career around engaging the students who hated school the most. In my classes my students are rewarded for asking, "Why do we have to learn this stuff?" This shows that they are concerned with their educations, and I'd better have an answer.

I consider teachers to be among an elite group of people who can truly change the world. I call it the ripple effect. Awhile back I was sitting around talking with a group of people who were in college in the early 1970s—a time of tremendous social upheaval and change. We were laughing about the protest marches, the campus takeovers, the hubristic attitude that by handing out leaflets, the world would slap its forehead and shout, "Of course, you're right! Why didn't I think of peace and love and feeding the children?" Instead, even after toppling an administration, it was business as usual. One person in the group shook his head at what naive fools we'd been, noting that not one of us had followed an idealistic path. I told him that I had: I'd become a teacher, and instead of trying to change thousands of minds at once, I was influencing people daily in a much smaller arena. And possibly my students would raise their children with slightly different attitudes about racism and sexism and their responsibility to the communities in which they live. It's like dropping a pebble in a pool. I can't change everything, but I can help my students at least examine why they believe what they do and to live a more deliberate life.

Teachers bear an awesome responsibility because a casual comment by a teacher will become part of a student's life script. How many times have you heard adults say that a teacher's encouragement influenced them to change the course of their lives? On the other hand, I know several adults who speak bitterly of a teacher who told them in 3rd grade that they were stupid or untalented or a waste of time, and they have never forgotten it. As teachers, we're not allowed to have such a bad day that we would take it out on our students. As teachers, we're closely watched role models who communicate more by what we do than by what we say. As teachers, we will be remembered forever. How we are remembered is up to us.

Louise Wigglesworth
9th–12th Grade Drama and Visual Arts Teacher
Pinelands Regional High School
Tuckertown, New Jersey
20 years

What they said

Louise Wigglesworth

This is a voice exercise for one or more actors. Different type styles are used to differentiate the plaintive voices of the students and sympathetic people in the community (italics) and the loud and raucous critics who don't take the time to look, listen, or understand (bold). The speaker/narrator's voice appears in plain text. The author uses this device to give, on the page, the same color to the voices that actors would give them in live performance.

Those who can't, teach. The others go to New York.

It's my first day as a public school teacher. I'm driving my brand new husband's brand new five-speed convertible down a long stretch of country road, which is deserted except for a woman wearing a babushka, a long skirt, and rubber boots. She's prodding a half-dozen cows before her with a tree branch. Neither she nor those cows have any sense of urgency. No, there's no question of passing them to get where I need to be. Inexperienced as I am with manual transmissions, I keep stalling out and starting up again behind those cows all the way to the little three-room school. Choking frustration, I cling to the words of a friend from theatre arts graduate school. What he said was, *Life puts you where you're needed the most.* So, I think: Is this it?

Nineteen years and four schools later, I think again. The friend's voice sounds with a thousand others in my head: the strident, the poignant, plaintive, exuberant, proud. Who could forget what they said?

How nice you're a teacher! If you have to work. . . . That's essentially a part-time job anyway, isn't it?

You teach what? Drama? So, you just sort of. . .have fun with the kids, right?

Drama? Do we still need that?

Well, yes, we need it. You see, something happens at its core, and it changes people.

Once, students, teachers, and parents had spent two months building a large and complex set for *Fiddler on the Roof*. At 9:00 a.m. on Saturday morning before our Thursday night opening, 50 of us arriving at school for our first full rehearsal with the pit orchestra find police cars and yellow tape everywhere. On stage, the 60-foot backdrop of Anatevka is crowbar-slashed, the walls of Tevye's house ripped and mangled, props smashed, destruction at every turn. Nothing is left whole, five days before opening night. I still hear the chorus.

Oh God. My tallis! Is it safe?

Who would do this?

*It's just a **story**. We're not **hurting** anyone.*

Unschooled in hatred, their terror resounds.

*Will they come again? Will they hurt **us**?*

Early Monday morning other voices counterpoint with power to turn the bitter lesson sweet.

Ahhh. . .yeah, Miss, I got some lumber here I'd like to donate. In fact, ahhh. . . my men and I can even stay for a few hours and ahhh. . .rebuild, that is, if you want. . . .

Hello. I'm Reverend Jennings. Some of my parishioners and I came over to do a little painting for you. See? We're dressed in our old clothes, ready to work.

Yeah, hi. This is Sam Peretti, the drama teacher from South River Regional. Hey, my students and I would like to come after school today and do whatever we can.

And then the voices of the academic critics.

What are you people doin' over there in 'at high school? How come you ain't teachin' those kids to read? All the taxes I pay an' 'ese kids can't read!

There's no way I'm going to pass Brit Lit.

Greg? A+? On your first paper for Mrs. Pell? What did you do?

Took a risk. You always told me, take a risk. I wrote an interior monologue for Beowulf, his thoughts, what he might have felt before he met Grendel, if there was any guilt, hesitation, fear. I just put myself in his place. She asked me where I ever got such an idea. I told her you make us do it every time we work on a character.

There's a dynamic that happens within a group of young student artists that makes teaching them quite thrilling. In some silent way, they recognize in each other their shared need to create. In my classes I have seen them lay down their so carefully constructed, present-day selves so that their historical selves can breathe and grow. And I have seen them learn to grant this grace to one another.

You see, something happens, and it changes people.

Hey, Joe. Where would you be now if not for your involvement in drama class and performances these last four years?

Oh, that's easy, man! Shootin' up, like the rest of my brothers.

In four years Joe went from at-risk student to nascent Shakespearean actor, set builder, young playwright, full scholarship winner. And still they ask.

Why can't these kids learn the way we learned years ago? If it was good enough for us. . . .

Rose: *Tell me about art, about myself: who I am, how I can survive when no one in my family talks to me. My mother died of an illness too shameful to name. I didn't speak to her before she died, or forgive her. Now my relatives think I caused her death. She died on the same day I found out I was the only one from this school who made All State Chorus. Did she have to take **everything** away from me? Now she visits my dreams, wanting me to come to her.*

Rose, have you talked to a counselor?

No. I can't talk about it.

Don: *My sister can't carry that stuff around with her anymore. I'm afraid for her. She needs to cry. Can I write it, the whole thing about our mother, in a play?*

And perform it in public? Don't you think that story is much too real and personal to put out there? Be careful. As their teacher you are responsible for any repercussions. This community does not want to hear about AIDS on our stage.

Oh. Well, okay. But. . .sometimes it's worth a risk.

"Broken Butterfly" the piece was called. There was a standing ovation and tears of both empathy and joy for this brother and sister who had used the stage to find their healing.

Julie, that new girl, man! She can sing and dance like an angel. She builds sets, does peoples' hair and make-up, everything! Where'd she come from?

I've been to 17 schools in my life. . .some of them private, she said.

Schizophrenia, her counselor said. *The "private" schools were institutions. See what you can do with her.*

Based on her amazing talent, real feel for character, we gave her the feature role in *Anything Goes*. Then came the string of excuses, the sore throats, the pulled muscles, the smoke screens.

*Julie, if you want a lead in one of our shows, you need to work the way we work here, which is to be prepared for **every** rehearsal and make it count, now.*

Oh, she had what it takes. But it was touch and go. On opening night Julie sat in the dressing room in her feathers and sequins, rocking back and forth and hugging a teddy bear.

This is the most important night of my life. I'm really scared, scared to death. But for the first time, ever, I didn't run away.

A rising star! Talent! Presence! She can probably go somewhere! they said.

She didn't run away, I said.

Until two weeks after the show when she disappeared, who knows where.

I wept for Julie, for Rose and Don, for all of them. I grow so tired, sometimes. It seems everyone else gets normal kids in their classes and I'm getting all the ones with problems. Where are the normal kids today?

*We **are** the normal ones now,* Greg said. *Please. Tell me about the theatre. I have the music in me already. Help me to know how to act. Help me to know my life.*

The educational system is bloated, is a failure, is hamstrung by government, by local interest, by unionization, is filled with disaffected students, teachers, custodians, bus drivers, lunch ladies. The educational system is. . .

. . .where miracles transpire every day. Do they know?

These classes are a waste! We need more technology!

Opening night of *The Crucible*. Jorge, still in John Proctor's costume, said, *You're really something. You made me do things I never dreamed I could do!*

Yes, Jorge. There's a word for people who do that sort of thing. It's *teacher*.

They come back to show off their grown-up, mature, in-control selves, educated, with goals, with a chance at a good life.

New York? I seem to be there. Tanya with her own young and ambitious production company, Ann a working actress, John training for the opera, Tom in musical theatre, Jackie a casting agency intern. Little bits and pieces of me all over New York. I never could have spread myself so far alone.

It's the morning of graduation. Greg, the soon-to-be conservatory student with the glorious singing voice, enters my office carrying a potted rose bush in riotous bloom, gorgeous, deep gold flowers, richly fragrant.

This is for you, for your garden, so you won't forget me.

Greg, as if I ever could.

My dentist said, **"You know, as I've gotten older I've truly come to appreciate you teachers and the intelligence of your career choice."**

Really? How wonderful!

Sure. You have summers off!

Susanne Rubenstein
9th–12th Grade English Teacher
Wachusett Regional High School
Holden, Massachusetts
22 years

Going Forward

Susanne Rubenstein

IT IS MID-AUGUST, AND I AM NOT sleeping well. I doze fitfully through the night, interrupted by dream voices that teeter on the edge of the familiar, and I awake heavy-headed, trying to uncover the cause of my anxiety. It's not entirely unusual, this late summer sleeplessness. I'm always somewhat unsettled by the approach of school. It is perhaps an occupational hazard for those teachers, fortunate as I, who can idle away the summer. Each year as September nears, I feel uneasy, already missing the freedom I'm soon to lose. Though I'm long past childhood, I still approach summer with childlike glee. Summer is for me a stretch of sun-streaked days, a time of novels and iced tea, long lunches with friends nearby, and letters to those far away. Each year I am loath to give it up, to return to early mornings, tight schedules, uncorrected papers, and stress. But something about this year is different. I feel like a prisoner waiting for the clang of the metal door behind me. The intensity of my disquiet concerns me, and so at night I lie awake.

I wonder if it's burnout—real burnout, the official version, the kind that makes me fear for my career as an English teacher. Certainly after more than 20 years of teaching it is a possibility, and I test myself for symptoms. I picture a pile of sophomore essays. I hear in my head the chatter of excited students. I create a conversation with a worried parent. None of these images makes me want to back away, so I make a diagnosis: It is not burnout. Still, there is a knot in my stomach as the August afternoons dwindle, and I feel helpless to prescribe a cure.

Then, in one of those curious spins of fate, two strangely similar things happen and the knot loosens. First is a letter, arriving in late August, my name and address penned in purple. I tear it open and a name from the past jumps out at me: Gina C. It's been years since I've seen her, my last memory being of a late-summer afternoon like this when I brought her a set of coffee mugs before she left for college. I skim the first paragraph. Gina of the long hair and outrageous opinions is in law school now in Washington, D.C. The letter is an impulse, prompted by a moment she took to look back through her high school yearbook. It's not unusual for me to keep up with ex-students, and though their letters may be sporadic, they allow me to watch my once-students grow and to feel that I'm helping them chart their course. But Gina is not someone I've kept up with these past six years. A young woman of independence, she didn't hold on to the strings of the past but forged straight ahead to the future, apparently with great success. She writes of travels out West and of the kinship she feels with the writer Pam Houston, a woman of courage much like Gina. She describes the challenge of law school, and then a line leaps out: *I now have a room of my own, a dog of my own, and a dream of my own—and I'm happy.* I feel a corresponding wave of happiness wash over me. I'm enormously pleased by Gina's success—and equally pleased that we have made a new connection and the start of an adult friendship.

And then there's Greg. Less than a week later, at a party, a tall blonde man approaches me. Though more than 15 years have passed since he sat in my classroom, I know him instantly; the grin he gives me as he hands me his business card from a Boston law firm has not changed. Proudly he introduces his wife and then launches into a tale of the terrors he wreaked in my classroom. Over dinner we reminisce, two friends sharing pieces of the past, the way it was in high school in the '70s.

"It's different now, isn't it?" he says, almost sadly.

I nod.

"Sometimes I wish I could go back." He smiles. "But we go forward, don't we?"

I finger his card and nod again.

Forward. That is where our students go and where we as teachers, if we remain passionate about our work, go, too, for our students take us with them. Gina and Greg reminded me of that. For me the joy of teaching is in the human connections that continue long after each school year ends. So in September, after nights of restful sleep, I gaze at my new classes full of gangly 15-year-olds, for whom the future seems forever away. But I know that it is not. Overnight they will turn into adults, marked by the moments we now share reading literature, writing journals, and exchanging ideas. Our time together changes each of us and makes us more than what we were, leaving the door open for a future when we may find each other once again.

the children

Kristie C. Wolferman
6th Grade Teacher
Language Arts Chair
Pembroke Hill School
Kansas City, Missouri
16 years

Students with Special Needs

Kristie C. Wolferman

ALTHOUGH THERE ARE SOME THINGS I don't like about teaching—the politics, the paperwork, the long hours, the grading, the lesson plans, and the stress—I love the students. Just ask my husband, my own children, and my friends, and they will tell you how much I adore my kids. I talk about how wonderful they are. Every year I have the best class I have ever had. Every year I have great students. Each one of them is a special challenge—a challenge I try to meet head-on. Over the years, but especially over the past 10 years as teachers have become aware of different learning styles, brain research, cooperative learning, cultural literacy, and a wide range of educational tools, I have become better equipped to deal with each child as an individual and to help each one develop to the best of his or her potential. Sometimes I'm successful; sometimes I'm not. However, there is nothing more wonderful than witnessing students learning something new. When I experience success in meeting students' needs and helping them become excited about learning, I realize how much I love teaching.

One year, the principal of the lower school where I teach 6th grade sent out a form to be filled out, as usual, ASAP. There were two columns. One was labeled "Student" and numbered one to five; the other was labeled "Special Needs." There were no instructions. So I just started writing.

First, I noted my "guardian angels" who, as educator and presenter Paula Wehmiller describes, are the students who keep us on our toes and provide us with that extra incentive to be as good as we can be in order to touch and maybe even reach them. My guardian angels included a behavior challenge, an academic challenge, and a couple of social challenges. The social challenges are a special worry because a teacher feels so powerless about being able to change other students' perceptions of a child or to make the outcast feel accepted. Then, too, teachers sometimes don't find socially wayward students very easy to talk to, or even to like. The guardian angel can then become the teacher's worst nightmare, as the instructor helplessly watches this social outcast become an academic failure and a behavior problem as well. I found my two social challenges to be really troubling, so I put them at the top of my list.

Then I added the children who showed attention deficit qualities but were either not diagnosed (except by me) or not medicated. Of course, I also had to list those students who had been labeled ADD (Attention Deficit Disorder) or ADHD (Attention Deficit Hyperactivity Disorder) and were medicated, but still needed help modifying behavior.

After that, I thought of the students with specific areas of academic weakness. By now I was well into my second page of names; a five-student limit was definitely out of the question. I listed students who couldn't write creatively, those who had test phobia, the dyslexic, the dysgraphic, and the one who has all the information in his head but just can't get it down on paper.

Now I realized I needed to list those students who were above the academic norm; they needed just as much attention as those below the norm. Several students needed enrichment in specific academic areas.

Of course, there also are well-rounded students, who really aren't a bit of trouble, but whom I've found learn best in very specific ways. In a class of 6th graders, these students are often the visual or kinesthetic learners, who perhaps have never shown their strengths until they, thanks to our new knowledge of multiple intelligences, were given opportunities to learn their individual ways. Those students certainly had special needs. By the time I had added the students who did not learn best in the traditional linguistic and logical modes, I found I had 34 of my 36 students listed (2 sections of 18).

Who was left? One young lady became number 35. She had a special family situation to which her teachers certainly needed to be sensitive. And the last student couldn't be left out because I realized that I had neglected her as soon as I saw her name standing alone as someone with no special needs. She was so perfect that she had never received extra attention, and that needed to be remedied. Perhaps she took her work too seriously. Did she ever have any fun? Now I was worried about the one student I didn't think had any problems at all.

I finally was finished with my six-page list of students with special needs, and I turned it in ASAP. Fortunately for some other teachers who are not quite as prompt as I, when I went to the office to turn my list in to the principal's box, he was standing there. I riffled through the pages to show him how long and complete my list was. He looked miffed. "That's not at all what I wanted," he muttered.

Irritated in return, since this had taken me quite a bit of time and thought, I snipped back at him, "You just read through this list and tell me who you'd like to have me take off." With that, I stomped out of the room.

The next day there was a memo in my box, in fact, in all the teachers' boxes, from the principal: "Forget about that 'Special Needs' list I asked you to make. I have just been reminded that all of our students have special needs."

Whatever the original purpose of the principal's "Special Needs" list, I felt fortunate to have had the exercise of writing it. It was a reminder to me that each child is special and unique, and it was a check to make sure I was meeting those needs. As I watched children that year succeed in areas in which they were experiencing difficulties—whether academic, social, or behavioral—it made me grateful that I had some small part in their successes. I revel in seeing my students learn to achieve, which is, to me, the special joy of teaching.

Todd R. Nelson
Head of Middle School
North Shore Country Day School
Winnetka, Illinois
18 years

clothes make the man

Todd R. Nelson

IN MY FIFTH YEAR OF TEACHING, MY class included a boy I'll call Max. Perhaps you know him? He wore a hat. In fact, Max was known as "The Hat Kid." He was inseparable from his leather, 10-gallon, pheasant-feathered cowboy hat. He was legendary: a pint-sized Pecos Bill right down to his Levis jacket and pointy cowboy boots; a diminutive young man who peered over large aviator glasses and always had his nose in a science fantasy novel. And he always, insistently, obstinately wore his hat. The hat was so large, it arrived before he did. His stubborn individualism was the source of amusement from teachers and derision from students: this pirate, this obstinate rebel, this Cat in the Hat. Thank goodness he was all hat and no cattle.

The school had a rule about hats. It went like this: "No hats." Whenever I asked him to remove it, within minutes the hat would reappear on his head, just like Bartholomew Cubbins. By October I was fed up with polite reminders about removing the hat as a way of dealing with the power struggle. Now it was about respect. But Max was perfectly capable of bringing to bear the full weight of the last thousand years of Western philosophy in his suit to be allowed to wear the hat continuously. He daily articulated the insidiousness of tradition, manners, and fashion versus individual rights as I invoked terms like appropriateness, decency, and clothing suitable to the occasion. My tactically inspired conversation about learning to pick your battles simply inspired Max to choose *this* as his battle. The showdown came: "Here we stand; we can do no other. If you don't take off that hat. . . ." In our meeting in the office of the Experienced and Reasonable School Head, détente prevailed. Max could wear the hat in the building but not during class. Win-win.

However, Max was not done teaching me a lesson, unbeknownst even to him.

At the parent conference the next week, Max's father commended the compromise strategy. "Stubborn isn't he!" he empathized. "He's a funny kid," he went on. "Did you know that he understands the concept of proportion? It's something that's very difficult to teach, even in graduate school. He comes to my office, looks at my architectural drawings, then gives criticism as to why certain features look askew. He's usually right. And I'm always amazed at what happens when we walk together through our neighborhood. He's on a first-name basis with everyone: the grocer, the laundry man, mail carriers, deli clerks. He's fascinated by other people and their work. When the power or telephone company has people working in a manhole, he stops to ask what they're doing. Everyone knows Max because he's inquisitive and has a genuine interest in other people."

So the kid in the hat had an intuitive sense of the golden mean. In a style beyond his years, he honored and connected with the other lives being lived in his city community. He knew the neighborhood and the neighborhood knew him, in personal, individual terms. While he may not have shared my sense of "choosing his battles," I had to admire his determination and powers of rational argument and outlook. In the present these qualities made his character appear stubborn; they were to become tenacity, self-confidence.

A friend of mine whose attorney son went through the "cowboy hat phase" says that you get the kids you need. In other words, if we listen closely, our children or our students are telling us not only who *they* are, but who *we* are. They bring us face-to-face with our former roles and elucidate some of the wonderful dilemmas and discontinuities of our own human development. We need this. And just when you think you understand the meaning of the costume, the child actor changes and becomes someone else, a whole new character.

Which leads me to admit there was something familiar about Max's sartorial flare. I recall my own 8th grade shopping trip to the Chess King store during which my mother patiently indulged my desire for chartreuse bell-bottoms and a purple butterfly shirt. "Are you *sure* you'll actually wear these?" was her only hint of reprobation, carefully disguised as pragmatism. "I will," I said. And I did. I also had a hat: a broad-brimmed, green fedora. I was quite groovy because I always, insistently, obstinately wore my hat. Looking back, I feel fortunate to have had parents and teachers who knew that I was a work in progress. Still am.

I do not know Max's present costume. Cowboy? Architect? Pilot? Did he run away and join the circus? But by December of that year he had switched to a discreet Air Force beret. I kind of missed the cowboy hat—because it was my hat, too.

Robin Alexandra Beach
Preschool Teacher, French Immersion
Washington International School
Washington, D.C.
15 years

Transparencies

Robin Alexandra Beach

IT WAS THE WINTER OF 1997 WHEN 15 3- and 4-year-old children and I discovered LIGHT. We touched light, caught light, manipulated it, measured it, and transformed our classroom into a world where light played everywhere and with everyone. We learned many wonderful words to describe the various transformations of light; we heard light in poems, and we found light in music, in water, in sand. We learned as much about what light does, and our wonder and delight in our explorations continue in our individual ways even now. Our school project itself lasted about six weeks.

In order to share our work with the rest of the school, we created a wall hanging, which we hung in a stairwell where everyone passes. We called this work "Transparencies." I attached mirrors to the wall behind the hanging so everyone could see himself or herself through it and experience firsthand what transparent means. Focusing so deeply on the tender and exciting exploration of the beauty in the world brought my students and me together in a profoundly rich and treasured experience. And it sprang from the children, not me.

This unplanned adventure started one day when Tatiana playfully began looking at everyone through the bottom of her plastic sandwich box. Soon the other children hurriedly ate their sandwiches, and they, too, looked through their boxes. With much delight and giggles they played. I asked them what colors their boxes were, and they didn't know what to say. We soon began discovering that some were easy to see through and some were not. I taught them transparent and opaque; our project was launched!

The next day, to welcome the children, I hung a large transparent glass ball over their tables. I placed transparent, translucent, and opaque pebbles and beads on our lighted "Table of Treasures." We listened to Debussy, Ravel, and Schubert while we put drops of colored ink into bottles of water, while we painted clear cellophane and clear bubble wrap, and while we caught colored water in clear plastic bags. Cloth can be a light catcher, too, and we put color on gauze and on cheesecloth. These cloths hung to dry all around our classroom, and we felt we were in a tent of light. We also danced with them.

We covered our windows with tissue paper collages and were made happy by the changing colors as the sunlight shone through them into our room and magically seemed to stick the lighted colors onto the rug, the tables, even our hands. At our sandbox we perceived that sand glistens and that when we looked closely at the grains of sand in the sunlight they transformed light into many different shapes. We drew these shapes. We blew through straws into soap and water mixed with paint and created tinted balls of light. We captured these light balls, preserving their shapes and colors by placing sheets of paper over them and popping the bubbles. I gave each child a pair of transparent protective goggles, which they wore everywhere they went in the school. One day we splashed water on them, and by looking at the light through the water on the goggles, the children were offered a distorted, fantastic view of things. One little boy found a rainbow in his.

I placed small mirrors in unexpected places: in the back of shelves, under their shiny metal wire sculptures, in the block corner. The children laughed when they came upon one by surprise and saw part of their own faces or the face of a classmate from across the room held in the reflection, held in the reflected light. Some of the stories we read seemed all wrapped up in the tactile light of make-believe, and the children discovered that some words sounded filled with light—some transparent, some opaque. Our curriculum objectives were all easily woven throughout our experimentations and explorations. With such involved students, all the sorting,

classifying, measuring, counting, comparing, coding, decoding, writing, and sequencing activities took on real and true meaning. As did this "Transparencies" project for all of us. We also became kinder during our cooperative learning journey. The nature of the project nurtured us into becoming patient, tolerant, and respectful of each other and all things.

This narrative provides but an overview of our work. To summarize its meaning for me, a teacher, I can loudly say that my sustained passion for teaching is found in listening, listening, and listening to the children!

Justine S. Heinrichs
6th–12th Grade String and Orchestra Director
Holland Hall School
Tulsa, Oklahoma
15 years

What Could Be Better?

Justine S. Heinrichs

WE BEGIN AT CHAOS. I REMEMBER being a 6th grader; or rather, I remember the fog. I remember the small bits I knew on the viola and the smug feeling that I could do something that others couldn't. Of course, everyone else in my class could do everything I could, but I wasn't counting them. I remember thinking I was pretty good. Given the amount of work I've done recently on intonation and rhythm, it's astounding I thought I could play at all.

A great thing about the becoming of musicians is their absolute confidence in what they know. They may not be able to shift, but they sure know how to play *Ode to Joy*. The students are always aware that there is another step in their development, but there is great satisfaction in the abilities they already have. I love that smugness in a beginning string player. Another great thing about becoming a musician is that one is always "becoming." There is no point of arrival. It is a lifelong sport. There is no time when a musician can say, "Well, I know all there is to know about that." So, musicianship reflects life, constantly evolving. Learning to play happens quickly. Improvement is apparent from the start. The evolution is immediately discernible and continues so throughout the journey toward wordless expression.

What could be better than giving a 6th grader something to be smug about (make that, proud of)?

Wordless but not amorphous. String students have concrete steps that must be taken in order to play. Like hiking in high altitudes, they take many small steps and never stop. Each step moves the players forward in their technique, and each small block of technique opens the door to new pieces of music. Students learn there is purpose to their efforts. Music is an expression in time. I tell my students that music is like a train. If one gets off, one must run ahead to get back on. In playing a piece that means moving one's eyes ahead and jumping back into the piece. If one takes time off, one must practice that much more to catch up.

We use our techniques to play music, and we play our music to teach ourselves how to deal with fear. Notice that I did not say conquer fear. One of the great gifts of performance is learning how to play even though one is afraid. Year after year nervous children perform before audiences, make their audible and inaudible mistakes, yet never give up. Courageous? Yes. But it's more than that. They play through their fear, in spite of their fear, and they learn not to succumb to fear. They learn that fear is natural and need not be debilitating. Through the years, each student becomes more confident in his or her abilities. Fear is never completely absent, but it can be controlled. Every once in a great while, the performers put themselves and their fears aside and go after the music. Then it's magic!

What could be better than teaching students that fear is manageable?

Great music can survive an inexperienced performance. I remember a review that once said, "Beethoven has survived worse. . . ." Masterful music can be played less than perfectly and still be a satisfying experience for both the listener and the performer. We play some popular tunes in my program, but Great Masters aren't called that for nothing. This "survival" factor illustrates that great music is bigger than words and abilities. Performance of this music or even arrangements allows the student to join "the music of the spheres." Although sensory, there is something about great music that lives outside the boundaries of our hearing. The student learns that the sound merely needs to be pulled out of the air like a rabbit out of a hat. Air doesn't seem so flimsy when one realizes that all the music of all the world resides in the invisible. There comes a time in orchestral playing when the harmonies vibrate in the chest and the performer is enveloped both inside and out by the music. The player is no longer a single entity but a part of the great beyond that only music occupies. The player cannot be more than himself, cannot play better than herself, and yet produces with others playing different—the same and similar—parts, this almost cosmic roar that is the whole-that-is-more-than-the-sum-of-its-parts. Every note I teach, every pattern, every rhythm is to serve this end so that my students will get a chance to experience this power.

What could be better than teaching students that their part is a precious contribution to the great whole-that-is-greater-than-the-sum-of-its-parts?

The listener hears music and sees in his mind's eye a beautiful summer day, lovers holding hands, or stars in the sky. The performer sees only the notes on the page. There is no time to think; rather, it is more like a conduit that is open, feeding the information through lightning-fast reflexes. The player exists only in the now, while aware of where he or she has been and is headed. This type of concentration requires absolute focus, absolute attention in each fraction of a moment.

What could be better than leading students through the minefield of a musical score so they can experience the heightened concentration that music has to offer?

A moment's flicker of concentration leads to that dreaded monster of performance, the mistake. Mistakes, though probably the most anxiety producing thought in a performer's mind, are actually among music's great blessings, and not only because we learn from them; rather, it is the ability gained to make mistakes and not be swayed from the course. A performer can only play in the now. It does no good to throw one's hands in the air in disgust. The whole group suffers. Years of performance teach that each mistake is minor; it is the reaction and recovery that make it horrific or inconsequential.

What could be better than teaching students that it is the response to mistakes and not the mistakes themselves that matters?

So, this is what I teach:
> You are special; be proud.
> Fear is manageable.
> The whole is greater than the sum of its parts.
> Work in the now.
> Forgive your mistakes.

What could be better?

Published with permission from Holland Hall School.

Patricia E. Wilson
K–5 Visual Arts Teacher
Harvard-Kent Elementary School
Charlestown, Massachusetts
25 years

Student Artwork and Excerpts

Patricia E. Wilson

Excerpt 1

Sonia. She never talks to me. Just stares intensely when I'm explaining or demonstrating a lesson. She never raises her hand to volunteer an answer or comment. Maybe she is still adjusting to the art room. She is new to our school this year. Maybe she is still trying to decide if I am really as stern as my teacher-facade appears to be.

Nice, overall design! Her watercolor is slightly thick, but these mixed colors are absolutely wonderful. Very warm. Really rich. Wait a minute. Sonia has little people living and playing in each and every letter of the word "friendship." Looks a bit like the gigantic Hollywood on the hill sign or, even better, a playground. Look at this little person playing on a swing suspended from the letter "p." I'm impressed with this artwork. These people are all interacting and having fun. Look at the little garden here in the right corner. Let's mark this one a "4" in every criteria area, get it up on the wall for display! This is a powerful visual statement that Sonia has created on a nine-inch square of art paper. She may not have raised her hand, but Sonia certainly did answer all my questions—superbly. And this is interesting. Most of the students independently decided to use circular designs in their squares. Sonia used a diamond shape. Really superb.

Excerpt 2

Stephen. In six years, I haven't quite decided whether Stephen is a budding minimalist, or if he is just plain slick. Rich, intense colors. Good, overall, circular design. He has synthesized the shape of the globe with the yin-yang symbol. (How many times will I have to see this ancient symbol this year?)

by Taylor Powers
Grade 4
Harvard-Kent
Elementary School

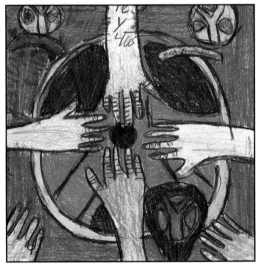

by Jessica Bailey
Grade 5
Harvard-Kent
Elementary School

The word "friendship" has been used to create a somewhat repetitive design pattern. Rich, warm tempera colors—nice application. Good, so far. Shapes, colors, linear details are very strong. The lettering could have been bolder—does not visually match the rest of the design. Maybe that is the sticking point. Stephen has successfully expressed friendship, but this lettering is visually weak! Should I mark this a 3 or a 4? And how much of this mental debate is based on my own designer bias for intricate, painstaking, almost rococo visual detailing? Enough! It's a 3.95!

Excerpt 3

Tricia is another very interesting individual. (Of course, each and every one of the 420 is interesting. Maybe one year there will be a group of students with no unique personalities or talents. They could all be the same. No individuality. No particular strengths or needs! No—too dull). Private school education until this year. Parents divorced. Mom, alone, could not afford the tuition. This is Tricia's first experience with "other people." It is obvious she is having a difficult time adjusting to the public school venue. Still has not really made friends. She is trying to find her place.

    Awesome design. Quite sophisticated! Tricia really understood the abstraction step of creating a symbol. The word "friendship" has been repeated in the shape of the peace symbol, which in turn is the shape of a face. Look at those two huge eyes staring out of the face. The background colors look like a rainbow. Wait! The rainbow actually defines a sky-to-sea space. Now, there could have been more fish in the sea. (There's that detail fetish, again. Tricia decided not to take my advice on that design issue. Good for her!) This is magnificently detailed work—especially for a 10-year old. Very strong colors—could have been more intense, but that's color pencils for you. What do I sense here? Serenity. No, not serenity. Those eyes are so demanding. But demanding what? I wish I could figure out the answer. I am moved by this piece of student artwork. It's a 4+!

Excerpt 4

These will be added to the wall exhibit today. I want to see some of my colleagues make a connection with some of this student work.

    I hear my next class arriving. I feel reinspired. I'm ready!

Lucienne Bond Simon
1st–3rd Grade Art Teacher
Hammond Eastside Primary School
Hammond, Louisiana
23 years

Dear Governor Foster

Lucienne Bond Simon

WHEN ARTS EDUCATION WAS THREATENED IN LOUISIANA, ARTS EDUCATOR and senior teacher Lucienne Bond Simon created a small, accordion fold-out "arts education primer" illustrated by her students. "Dear Governor Foster," shown in miniature on the next two pages, uses questions and drawings to illustrate what would be lost without funding for the arts: "Who will design your car? Who will plan our bridges? Who will be a movie star?" The case and its presentation were so compelling that arts funding was restored.

If arts funding is not protected

Dear Governor Foster,

BEGIN HERE

Who will design your car?

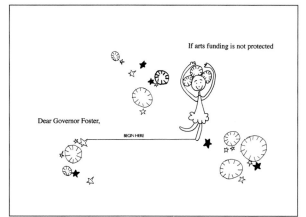

Who will plan our bridges?

Who will be a movie star?

Who will make good music?

Who will dance at a *fais do-do*?

Who will write "You Are My Sunshine"?

Who will decorate The Mansion?

Who will lift your spirits
when you're low?

Who will take your photo?

Who will make sure your coffee mug
Fits your finger just so?

Who will draw the picture
On your next birthday card?

Who will plan the garden
In your Franklin home backyard?

Please, dear Governor Foster,
Don't chop at rock and roll
Or Bach or Neil Simon
Or ballets that touch our soul.

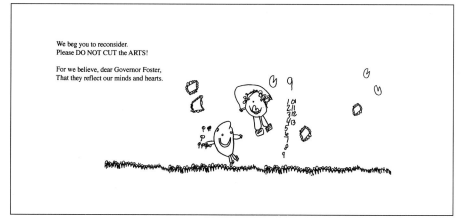

We beg you to reconsider.
Please DO NOT CUT the ARTS!

For we believe, dear Governor Foster,
That they reflect our minds and hearts.

Lois Marie Harrod
9th–12th Grade English Teacher
Voorhees High School
Glen Gardner, New Jersey
33 years

This Is a Story You Already Know

Lois Marie Harrod

This is the story of the high school student,

who drove from Pennsylvania to Vermont,

and the story of the loud fat girl

who worked with him at Burger King,

the one who said, *how like him,*

not to shoot himself and spoil his pretty face,

and the story of her skinny friend

who agreed, *yea, handsome son of a bitch,*

combing his hair in the french fries,

and the story of his mother

who drove the school bus

and had to watch the blue-eyed boys

alive and laughing at every stop

and this is the story of one of them

who also hooked up a tube to the exhaust

of his father's car and sat there a long time

thinking, but did not turn on the engine,

and this is the story of his coach who thought

the one who died was still a pain in the ass

and said so at the funeral, and the story

of the English teacher who wished

he had waited for the lilacs

as if beauty ever had any power to save,

and this is the story of the girl

who believed if she had not blown him off

that last time when he called her from Rutland,

he might still be living, and the story

of his friends who said she did kill him,

the story of how sometimes

she got drunk and wanted to kill herself

and her new boyfriend said, *no, no,*

nothing could have stopped him, but she couldn't believe,

and this is the story of the last words

a hundred people heard him say,

the kid he bought dope from, *stuck, man,* and the boss

who had finally fired him, *fuck you,*

and the cafeteria lady, *three meatballs please,*

father, son and holy ghost,

and his next door neighbor,

hi-ya Mrs. Erlington,

sexy dress you have on today,

he was always flirting, that one,

and this is the story

of his sister who cried in her bedroom,

the girl who wouldn't wash the shirts

she had taken from his closet

and had worn as her own that week between

the day he fought with his father and left

and the day the telephone began to ring.

Nette Forné Thomas
9th–12th Grade Art Teacher
Art Chair
Arts High School
Newark, New Jersey
35 years

Fallen from Grace

Nette Forné Thomas

The late bell had rung, and students had already seated themselves at their respective seats in my art room. The usual buzz of preclass conversing among groups of friends ensued. An air of expectancy nonetheless was evident. It was not usual for them to have this much time to themselves before being given directions for the day's activities.

I, myself, did not anticipate the extended delay a few minutes earlier when I conceded to listen to the student who approached my desk and quietly stated, "Mrs. Thomas, I got to talk to you."

I looked up, seeing a student from the year before enrolled again in my art class. I knew him to be a perfectionist, always seriously questioning the correct application of the most minuscule detail. However, I was also aware that on more than one occasion he used the pretext of needing artistic advice as a means of gaining access to the project room behind my desk. He would quickly sidle through the open doorway, intently peruse his reflection in the large mirror, and adjust a collar or brush his hair with the palm of his hand before retrieving his artwork and presenting it for criticism.

Anticipating a question about his assignment, I nodded my acquiescence, waiting for him to get his work. He looked a little puzzled because I did not move from my desk. In a lowered voice that pleadingly relayed a sense of urgency, he added, "In private, please?" I looked up from the roll book, focused on his face, and read in his eyes and manner an uncharacteristic nervousness.

We stepped into the smaller room. I closed the door. He propped both elbows on the counter, burying his head in his hands. As he slowly raised his head, brushing one hand over his face, he repeated the need to talk. Expressing his feeling that he could confide in me, his belief that I would not tell anyone if he asked me not to, his eyes pleaded for this assurance. A kaleidoscope of the many classroom discussions engaged in last year flashed through my mind. Remembering caused me to hesitate. How great the contrast—this agitated worried boy-child now, then a premature, posturing man-of-the-world, oozing with the cocky self-assurance of one who is "getting over" on the authorities.

In the relaxed atmosphere of that small studio art class he exuded brash bravado—hinting at deals, projecting get-rich schemes, and contemplating questionable involvements. Our viewpoints frequently clashed as he boasted confidence in his ability to out-talk, out-maneuver, and outwit "them." Cautioning him not to underestimate those he chose to pit himself against, I forecast a future of close encounters and eventual pitfalls. Then he rejected the possibility of this premise. I remembered; I was reminded; I hesitated. I did not want to hear that the possibility was now a reality. Waiting, the boy-child behind the eyes of troubled youth still sought my reassurance. I gave it.

His need to talk to someone was indeed overwhelming. He detailed the criminal involvement, the imminent threat of apprehension, the paralyzing fear of not knowing what to do now. Inwardly, I sighed with relief for my worst fear had not materialized. He was in no danger of bodily harm, nor had he injured another. I could now admonish, give practical advice. Most importantly, I could hope to penetrate those inner recesses I was unable to reach last year. This unfortunate, unsuccessful, thwarted criminal act was now the chink in the armor—that armor of youthful brashness, of cocky self-confident superiority borne of ignorance. It was a failure that provided a wedge I could use in an attempt to dislodge the false façade. I probed with a fervent, tenacious sincerity rooted in desperation. I attempted to reach out beyond the immediate travail, to affect the child in order to save the man-to-be. I tried.

I hope for success. Yet, I feel strangely burdened—perhaps because I can enlist no other aid for him, certainly not the "proper authorities" or his father, who should know. I can't tell. I gave my word.

Postscript

"Fallen from Grace" recounts an actual incident. At the story's conclusion, one could initially perceive the event as a depressing commentary that focuses on the negative life situations teachers encounter and about which they can do little, or nothing. Upon reflection, it becomes apparent that quite the opposite is the case. The student, who at first appeared to pay no attention to the advice I gave in class, evidently respected my opinion. Because of this I was able to prevail upon him to confide in his father despite the reaction he feared. While his father definitely and sternly reprimanded him, he was able to intercede, thus preventing this one mistake from leading to others. This gave the student a "second chance," which can make a life of difference.

The story and its postscript vividly emphasize the two reasons I continue to love to teach. I don't teach a subject; I teach children. And I've seen the difference a teacher can make.

The Ambiguities of Chokers, Lifelines and Safety Nets

Nette Forné Thomas

The Ambiguities of Chokers, Lifelines and Safety Nets is a work commenting on the idea that what adorns can also restrain, what can be latched onto for security also holds one close. It is watercolor and scratchboard from a series entitled "Woman's Struggle."

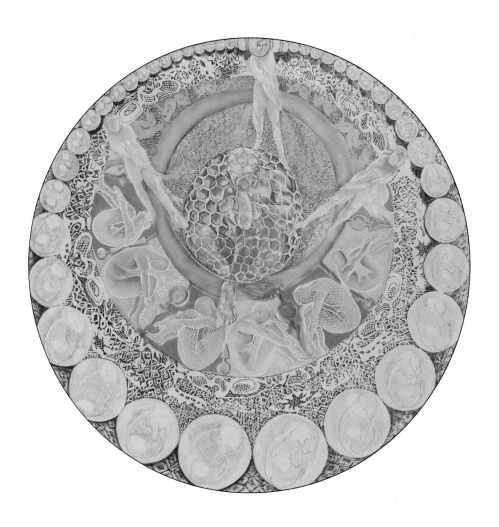

Irene E. McHenry
Teacher of Teachers
William Penn Charter School
Philadelphia, Pennsylvania
21 years

Passionate Community

Irene E. McHenry

ONE RAINY DAY, KRISTIN, FULL OF unbounded 8-year-old energy, got the idea that the halls in our new school would be great for roller skating. In this school, which we were creating from scratch, every idea was valid for consideration. The other students and I could immediately see Kristin's vision: children on roller skates speeding up and down the long, glossy, linoleum-tiled halls of the insurance company building where we rented space during the first years of the school. What I learned with visceral love and excitement from those days, 20 years ago, is how the spark of a child's idea could ignite the community because it was honored and valued and engaged and wrestled with by the community.

Kristin brought her idea to the morning meeting where we discussed every aspect, ramification, and issue that we could see associated with it: safety, fairness, work interruption, motivational value, fun. The system we collaboratively designed, incorporating both a values discussion and a math lesson, was a rotating, two-at-a-time, turn-taking system with 10-minute turns throughout the day. After the meeting, the excitement in the air was palpable. We hummed through that day.

The next morning, small, silver, clip-on-the-shoe skates and occasional pairs of white or black shoe skates were lined in neat, orderly rows outside each classroom doorway. We made a chart on the wall, with names indicating the turns. The day flew by as children quietly, by twos, left their work areas for 10-minute skates in the hall, returning with high spirits and adrenaline rushing to a keen focus on their classroom tasks. There was no inattention. There was high motivation from anticipation or from satiation.

(In retrospect, I offer this kinesthetic solution as an alternative to Ritalin or Dexedrine for attention disorders today.) Fortunately, everyone had a turn, and we were on our second rounds before a man from the insurance company offices at the lower level of the building came to investigate the source of the strange and constant rumbling sound and put the brakes on the skating project.

Daily, we found something new to be passionate about, and I carry this intention forward into my work today. Some bright new twist for how to do "school" was constantly being added by students or parents or teachers. Without difficulty, we had what would now be called an inclusive classroom: two ESL (English as a second language) students, one EMR (educable mentally retarded) student, and many "gifted and talented" students, if we had used public school classifications. We created a learning community where each person's strengths were valued, honored, and employed and where each person's difficulties and vulnerabilities were not an isolating factor. We worked in cross-age groups and varied those groups from time to time. We kneaded and baked bread, wove collaborative art on a four-harness loom, picked wild violets and made violet jam, built a rabbit classroom in a patch of clover in the school yard, wrote and directed plays, designed and made costumes, sewed and painted and counted and sang and read and measured and cooked and imagined.

What I learned as a teacher during five years in that new, constantly evolving school is that when you pay attention to every child's idea, every moment is a teachable moment; every question is a journey to be taken; every curiosity is a window to the universe. It does not surprise me that many students from the early years of the school have become teachers. They knew the excitement of engaging with their own ideas and the ideas of others to create something new; to learn something new; to open a wider view of possibility; to explore the vast territory of the unknown, the emergent, the infinite.

Death, the great teacher for those of us who still have the gift of human potential, has come to three of the students from the founding years of the school, cutting their lives short in early adulthood: Jimmy by a fraternity house fire, Ming by lupus, Kristin by depression and suicide. I recently spent time with Kristin's mother, an inspirational elementary school art teacher. We remembered together Kristin's enthusiasm for creative projects, her abundance of new ideas, her love of motion, her role in shaping the early days of the school. I felt honored to have witnessed and midwifed the birth of Kristin's and her classmates' ideas, to have witnessed their growth and development and to know that their lives, my life, and the lives of others were changed as a result of the creative passion kindled in our years together. That experience honed my understanding and present practice of teaching as an art of building passionate community.

Cultural Perspectives

Lanie Higgins
6th Grade Science Teacher
McCall Middle School
Winchester, Massachusetts
20 years

Color Blind

Lanie Higgins

DENISE AND I WERE IN ONE OF OUR deep discussions about our teaching experiences late one afternoon when we began to describe our most memorable students. "It's a shame," said Denise, "that everyone couldn't view the world through Peter's eyes."

"Who's Peter?" I hadn't recalled Denise's mention of this particular student before.

"Peter was such a great student," Denise began. "He was my first METCO* student. I can remember how shy he was at the beginning of the year because this was an entirely new school experience. The Boston Public Schools matched his profile in a Dorchester kindergarten with our school environment and thought this would be an excellent suburban setting for him.

"I remember Peter entering my room that first day not knowing what to expect. But as soon as he saw that the other students were new to 1st grade and also learning about the building and schedules, he eventually joined into all the activities. As the year went on, I realized Peter was a promising, bright student. He read constantly and won first prize in several Trivial Pursuit contests Mrs. Driscoll organized in the library. I planned to share this with his mother during our first parent conference.

"Peter's mother was unable to attend an earlier conference because it was difficult for her to travel from Boston and keep her work schedule. I was so looking forward to this meeting. However, when his mother arrived, she just stared at me in such amazement that I felt uncomfortable. I started to explain Peter's progress and she suddenly interrupted: 'My God. You aren't black. You aren't one bit black,' she glared at me. 'The way my Peter speaks about you, I thought for sure you were black.' Peter's mother contin-ued to stare at me in disbelief.

"I really didn't know how to reply. I began to describe Peter's achievements, which were obviously falling on deaf ears. I ended the conference rather awkwardly."

Denise paused and then continued, "The next day I received a call from Peter's mother. 'I am so sorry,' the apologetic voice began, 'but I was shocked when I saw you because I just assumed that you were black. All these months I had pictured this wonderful black woman, this wonderful black teacher, who opened my son's eyes to the world through reading. All he has talked about is his school, his teacher, and his books. He loves you so much I thought you were black. When I asked my son to explain why he never told me you were white, Peter looked at me and simply stated, *Ma, she might be white on the outside, but I just know she's black on the inside.* Well, I thought, my boy is seeing the world where I have truly been blinded.'"

Denise and I continued to sit in silence, thinking about this little boy's ability to communicate the integration of his experience. Physical characteristics were not important; sharing the experiences of the heart mattered.

We returned to our cars, said our good-byes, and knew remember-ing students like Peter is the reason we keep teaching.

* METCO refers to Metropolitan Council for Educational Opportunity, a City of Boston program providing opportunities for inner-city children of color to attend suburban schools in the Greater Boston area.

Rose Ratteray
4th–8th Grade Media and Technology Teacher
P.S. 22
Jersey City, New Jersey
22 years

Unplanned Lessons

Rose Ratteray

I'VE ALWAYS WANTED TO BE A TEACHER. After graduating from college, I began teaching in an inner city elementary school in the South Bronx. I remember my feelings of hope and idealism, the sense that I could make a difference in a child's life and really elevate the total child. During my years of teaching I've had many meaningful and lasting experiences; here are two of them.

It was the first day of my very first job. I wore a lovely white blouse with a Peter Pan collar, a blue skirt, stockings, and pumps with a small heel so I would not tower over my students. The class was great because there were only 12 children. While I was telling the children what they would need and what a great year we were going to have, several additional children arrived. As the morning progressed, more and more children came until, by 11:00 a.m., I had run out of desks, chairs, and space. I attempted to make up an attendance card and discovered I had over 45 students in my class. I took them to lunch and went to the office to notify the principal. She laughed and said the number was accurate. In fact, she was attempting to balance the classes, so I might get a few more students. I told her it would be difficult to meet the needs of so many children. Again she laughed, saying I was not hired to meet the needs of children, just to teach. I went home thinking: "So this is the real world of teaching." I remained at the school for two years until a "great fiscal crisis" in the city led to the layoff of 10,000 teachers and municipal workers, including me.

As a new teacher, I had tons of energy and optimism, and it was not long before I found another position. Although in a large city, this elementary school did not fit the stereotype of the failing inner city school. While families had low incomes, they had the same aspirations as middle income families. Students were motivated, parents were actively involved, and the school was a pleasant place to teach.

As one of only three African American teachers, I felt responsible for blending Black history into my curriculum. In late January, I started to prepare the students for Black history month. I told my students my contribution was going to be a name change. I had gone to the library, poured over history books, and researched the origin of African names. After days of study, I chose a name that suited me and reflected my origins, or so I thought. I decided I would wait until the first Monday in February to present my new name to the class.

Monday arrived. I dressed in my fanciest African outfit and eagerly faced my students. After our opening exercises, I would typically greet the children by saying: "Good morning, my good students." They loved it when I said "my good students." This day I said, "Jambo," Swahili for good morning. They looked at me oddly. I told them I was using an African greeting, and they could respond Jambo, or good morning. Since this was a class that loved learning new things, they were excited to learn the greeting. I explained that I had changed my name to reflect my heritage. My new name would be Banabakhe. We went over the pronunciation a few times, and they became quite comfortable with it.

The following day the children called me Mrs. Banabakhe; I answered, and we continued to work. The next day, a few children called me by the new name, but most quietly resumed calling me Mrs. R. By Friday, the entire class was back to calling me Mrs. R. Because I didn't make an issue of it, they continued calling me that name.

More than a week passed and class proceeded smoothly. The following week, a parent came to see me about a minor matter. When she greeted me, she seemed hesitant. I asked if anything was wrong. She replied that her daughter told her I had an African name, but she didn't remember it and she didn't know how to address me. I told her not to worry, just to call me Mrs. R., as all the children had returned to doing. She breathed a sigh of relief, and we had a productive conversation.

When I returned to my students, it occurred to me that I didn't remember my African name. I went to my desk to look up the name but couldn't find it. Frantically, I began searching among all of the papers. Then I asked the students, who looked at me blankly and finally replied: "You're Mrs. R." When I told them I meant the African name from two weeks before, they said they didn't remember either. A few brave souls even tried to give me a new African name. A student from the Ivory Coast gave me several fitting names, but I wanted the original name I had found. Their homework that evening: find my name. At dismissal, they assured me someone would find it, and we would all learn the name again.

School began the next day with an air of amusement in the classroom. It was funny, after all, to think that I had "lost" my name. After opening exercises, I said: "Jambo, children." To my surprise, they replied in an African tongue: "Good morning, beautiful teacher." The child from the Ivory Coast had taught them the words in her language. Elated, I changed the morning plan so that we could fully use the lesson I had just learned: that we often attach too much importance to a name, especially when we are trying to prove a point. In my quest to have students identify me with my culture, I had lost the reason I was using an African name. During the discussion, the class and I came to the conclusion that many of us who use hyphenated names frequently do so out of a need to have our heritage recognized and respected. The lesson became multidimensional: I was able to incorporate civics, literature, and geography to teach them how vital each ethnic group is to our country. I was also showing them that in my quest to prove something, I was guilty of overkill. The issue was not the African name, but my method of using it.

The lessons learned that day stayed with me and my students. Over the course of a few years, parents of different nationalities would comment on my sensitivity to their children's backgrounds. The students in that original class were pleased because I ended the lesson with humor. I told them that whenever they wanted to address me using my African name, they could call me Ms. Bella Bella because that was easy to remember and was just words. Several students went home and told their parents. The Italian, French, and Spanish families sent messages indicating what Bella meant so the children were, in effect, saying Ms. Beautiful Beautiful!

When I think of teaching, I recall great classes like that one and how eager students are to learn. I recall the support of parents who want to be part of the child's education. Whenever I meet a former student and we reminisce, I think of how fortunate I have been to have taught such great students and to have been a part of their lives for a brief time. So many—students and parents—have taught me and enriched my life.

I began teaching to make a difference in the lives of children. Now that I have taught for more than 20 years, I realize how naïve I was. I understand that teaching is a two-way street. Although I am the teacher, I am also the student. Teaching has changed me.

Lessons and Lives

Robert L. Bibens

MY FIRST THREE YEARS IN THAT central Oklahoma public school classroom were a strange combination of memorable, educational, and awkward. I'd been assigned a room full of 5th graders for whom I resembled more of an older brother than an authority figure; only about 11 years separated their ages from mine.

The day before classes began, the principal announced to the faculty that we were to contact each student's parents sometime in the first week to arrange a convenient opportunity to drop by, spend time introducing ourselves, and share our hopes and dreams for the coming year. I was able to reach about three-quarters of the families, but since a good number had no phone, I was forced to drive out to their homes to make a cold-call visit.

Everything was going fine. Parents were politely enduring my nervous conversation; I had sampled cookies and lemonade innumerable times. One of the last houses on my list, however, caught me completely off guard.

There was no door in the doorway. A blanket hung limply in its place. In my mind's eye the image of the coming winter wind blowing furiously past that piece of cloth made me shudder, even though it was still September. Without a doorbell, I searched momentarily for the proper place to knock; I chose the wooden doorframe. Mrs. G. pulled back the blanket and, smiling broadly, welcomed me into their home. As I entered, I surveyed my surroundings and gulped hard in order to disguise my shock. I'd always heard that a dirt floor could be packed down solid, but I'd never experienced that firsthand. This floor was completely smooth, even shiny— worn to a natural sheen by thousands of footsteps over time. The living area was meager, at best, but neatly kept. A big soft couch and an easy chair were the only pieces of furniture. A cane rested in one corner.

Mr. G., I later learned, had been wounded in the Korean War. He had never been able to find full-time employment upon his return. His wife worked two jobs and had done the lion's share of raising their six children—seeing that meals were on the table, clothes were clean, and homework finished. Each of the children present that day was well mannered, intelligent, self-motivated, articulate, and neat as a pin. The oldest son had just graduated from the Naval Academy, and they were proud to show me a photograph of their college-age daughter, who was on scholarship at Duke University.

I was still struggling with my reactions to the surroundings when Mrs. G. surprised me with an invitation to stay for dinner. Before I could politely refuse, I found myself sitting at the table holding hands with one of the little boys while Maria, my student, offered thanks. I'm not proud of it, but while everyone else was praying, I was wondering if dinner would be something familiar and, even more importantly, whether I should be taking food out of these mouths when every dollar obviously counted so much.

Dinner was terrific. The discussion and family banter were lively. Smiles were abundant. Little did I know that after I left that evening all of the children would strip down to their underwear. Momma would wash the one outfit that belonged to each child, hanging it on the line to dry before morning. Homework would be done—every night through high school—with all the children sitting around the kitchen table in their underwear so that they would have clean clothes to wear the next day.

On my way home, having experienced such universal and unconditional acceptance, I had to wonder: Who had been the teacher and who the student that evening? I had gone over to give the family something of myself but had returned home full of all that they had given me: new perspective, some shattered stereotypes, and an appreciation for the many blessings that had so easily come my way.

Robert L. "Bert" Bibens
K–8th Grade Chaplain
Holland Hall School
Tulsa, Oklahoma
11 years

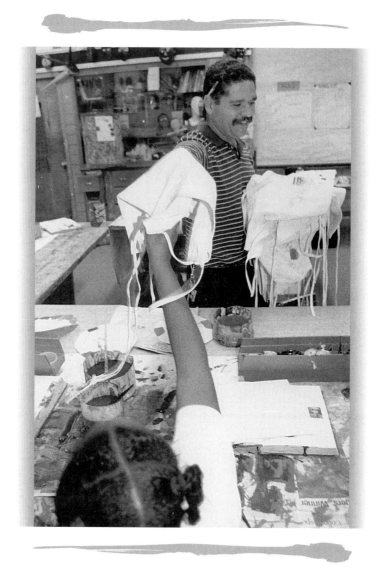

Fausto Sevila
6th–8th Grade Art Teacher
Luis Muñoz Marin Middle School
Newark, New Jersey
15 years

The Problem with Adam and Eve

Fausto Sevila

Their aspiration lacked imagination
they only had each other
no old stories to tell
to compare

No grandmother
dropping white feathers
from her pillow head
on their careless path
Saying: "*Ven aqui*
Do you know you have your father's eyes?"

No grandfather history of
listening to baseball games
drinking expresso *con un buen tabaco*
in the late afternoons
while throwing a *casco* against the brick wall

No Felipe,
No Alfreda, Masaccio or Wilfredo Lamb
They were not a part of your history
It's not your fault
We are all malnourished in some type of
purity
and not enough diversity

I don't hold against you
that Andy Warhol adored you
with his pretentious plastic simplicity
naïve chicken shit white hair bread appropriations
and boring lines

His work
After all
Adds to the gene pool

With all of this diversity
you can look down in glory

not shame

Look down and
realize the fruit to be
an ovary
a testicle
maybe even
one of god's many eyes

or a test to see
how fast you can forgive
yourselves

A revelation that
dis-obedience is at the center of creativity

ripping the fruit off
the tree and eating it
was a reaction

an unimaginative act

If they would have talked to someone
from Cuba
Puerto Rico
Santo Domingo or India
You might have realized that the fruit
is a mango
That you should never tear a mango off the branch
while it's still green
or sitting
on its branch

The bitterness will only sting you
like a bee on the tip of your tongue

It's not your fault you never ate Pucha's
garbanzos with pig's feet stew
black bean soup
con *arroz blanco y onions crudo*

It's not your fault
you have never seen cars from Bellville
making roller coaster doughnut-shaped tiremarks
in the middle of desperate
lonely streets

I forgive you for your monolingual imagination
and your *Ingles* only slogans
I know things were simpler then
and it's not your fault

Lend me your stomach
my fellow
Eva y Adam
and let's imagine a rich garden
With ten thousand gods
Ten thousand species with every
spoken word
Ten thousand worlds in one city

Some one would have
advised you to
sit

Ask

ask for the mango

Sit and wait

Invent painting while
writing what you see

You will notice
the green sliding into magenta
red flowing into orange

Respect grows when paying close attention

Walk around
the mango sculpture
imagine you are satellites orbiting earth

The mango like a large head
will drop
it always does
next to your feet
if you are patient

Promise not to rip it off again

then
eat quickly while it's still sweet

How do you teach waiting?

Arrogance
imposes its will
and rules out
whole species

It's all very clear to me
I cannot afford to think
that I know

who you are

When I question:
What keeps me enthused as a teacher?
Can the answer be
It is the mystery that every person is

Is it your face
or the tree
I am trying to see
in
you
and
the fruit
I want to eat?

Margaret M. Wong
9th–12th Grade Teacher of Chinese
Director of International Education
Breck School
Minneapolis, Minnesota
28 years

Peaches and Plums

Margaret M. Wong

I REMEMBER AN AUGUST EVENING IN Nanjing in 1949, the close of a perfectly ordinary day. My parents returned home early from a party. My father woke the other younger children and me and gathered all 8 of us, ages 1 month to 15 years of age, around him. He told us we had to leave China, that very night, for an indefinite period of time.

We had been a family of privilege and security, accustomed to servants and deference, but now we had to flee the advancing Communist army and abandon anything we couldn't carry with us: our home and its furnishings, most of our possessions, our cars, and my father's real estate holdings. And of course it was obvious that all his investment stocks were about to become worthless.

His message to us that night was brief, but very powerful: Although we were about to lose everything, all our money and material property, even our very country, the one thing that no one would ever be able to take from us was the knowledge in our heads. In later years, I appreciated the fact that he was speaking from his own life, as the barefoot country boy who, at age 11, had walked to the schoolmaster in the nearest village and begged to be educated.

His statement that August night in the penetrating heat of a Nanjing summer evening has had a profound impact on me. It motivated me to study diligently, and it directed me to the choice of teaching as a career. From this childhood trauma and my father's calm and wise words, I was privileged to learn early in life that knowledge and learning are not just the provenance of scholars and technicians. They are not simply a way to get the best jobs. Knowledge and learning are truly the greatest personal wealth and the surest possession. And what could be a better use of one's time, energy, and spirit than teaching, making knowledge accessible to young people and conveying to the new generation my father's message, with the hope that children yet unborn will teach it to their heirs.

Now, as I look back on 25 years of teaching Chinese to American kids, I am mindful of a Chinese proverb referring to the rewards of teaching:

桃李滿天下

"Peaches and plums all over the world."

"Peaches and plums" refers to the hundreds of students I have taught who now are doing interesting and meaningful things all around the world. Who are they? When they started Chinese, they were always asked the difficult question: "Why are you taking Chinese? What good will it do you?" If I didn't ask them myself, I knew that sooner or later parents or friends or great aunts would challenge them. I have answers for them, of course. You couldn't teach such an "exotic" subject for all these years without having some answers to those questions. But the truth is that my answers are provisional and temporary because each student really discovers the answers on his or her own.

What have some of those answers been?

There are the scholars: the Ph.D.s and doctoral candidates who have done significant work in areas as diverse as correlations of Chinese and Western medicine, comparative literature, the contemporary democracy movement, the historic patterns of the spread of diseases from China to Japan, and the quality of marital relationships in contemporary urban China.

There are the teachers: those who teach English in China (and inevitably a perspective on our country), or those who bring to their teaching of any subject a heightened world context and those who come back to my classroom as tutors and assistants.

There are the agents of enlightenment: the head of the Ford Foundation programs in China, the administrators of exchange programs, environmentalists specializing in China, human rights activists, even a fellow who organizes ornithological tours between China and the United States.

There are the practitioners of business or law, here or in Asia, who build ties of commerce and understanding between our countries.

There are the health care professionals, both the medical doctors trained in the Western tradition and the practitioners of traditional Chinese medicine.

There are even entertainers: the models, the pop stars of Chinese television, and "Captain Tim," the traffic reporter for Taipei radio!

And there are many students, perhaps the majority, who have not chosen a career focused on China but have "only" brought to their chosen fields an extraordinary appreciation for the richness, depth, and subtleties of the differences between China and the United States and, by extension, of any two cultures. They surely have not benefited less than the others from their encounter with China and the Chinese language.

So many peaches and plums! But let me tell you about one more, a student who brought me special pride. I remembered "Charles" as a difficult student, somewhat rebellious, always testing the limits of acceptable classroom behavior and not especially diligent in his studies. I keep up with many former students, but I was a little surprised when Charles telephoned and suggested lunch. He had just graduated from college with a double major in Chinese and English. We had a pleasant chat. I asked him what he planned to do next. He replied without hesitation: He had thought about it a lot and had decided that he couldn't think of anything more worthwhile than teaching. He wanted me to know that.

青出于藍

"*Green comes out of blue*," says the old Chinese proverb. The mark of a good teacher is to be surpassed by your students. And so, in the Chinese expression, I have often had the satisfaction of watching students bathed with the teacher's "blue" light slowly begin to emit their own light in the "purer" and more intense green.

on Teaching

Dianne H. Close
7th–12th Grade Classics Teacher
The Winsor School
Boston, Massachusetts
24 years

Play by Play

Dianne H. Close

An ETC Sports Special
Frank Farrell, Announcer,
Dan Dewey, "Color" Man

[Theme Music: "Pomp and Circumstance" or "Gaudeamus Igitur"]

[Cameras pan assembled crowd and nearly empty playing field, then switch to the two sportscasters wearing headphones and blue blazers in their broadcast booth.]

Announcer: Well, Dan, it's a big night for our fans, isn't it? Give us some background on what we're going to see.

Color Man: Right, Frank, it's going to be the Match of the Century. Mrs. Close, the outstanding 20-year veteran teacher, who has been named the MVT 6 times in the last 8 years, will be up against one of the toughest fields ever—a 9th grade, second year Latin class of heterogeneously grouped girls who have just two weeks left before final exams.

An: And tell us about the venue, Dan.

CM: This is really a very tough arena. It's the third day of an unprecedented heat wave, in an un-airconditioned school, with only two days left before the Memorial Day long weekend.

An: Well, Dan, let's look at the playing floor. The class is coming in now. I'd say they are *thoroughly* warmed up! What's the temperature down on the court right now?

CM: Well, it's almost noon—(did I mention that this is the class before lunch?)—and the temperature on the floor is 98 degrees Fahrenheit. It's actually cooler *outside*.

An: Unbelievable! Oh no, you don't think they might. . .

CM: . . .demand to be taken outside? No, Frank, I doubt it. Close is known for hating the grass. She can play on grass, but she considers it a giveaway. She only uses that tactic as a surprise move when she knows she is winning anyway.

An: Dan, tell us about this player with the two little ponytails on either side of her head. She looks hot and tired *and* mad!

CM: Yeah. That's Dulcey. She's new on this team and has really become a major playmaker. See how she's chewing gum?

An: Whoa, she *is*!

CM: Yeah, she's a champ. Last year she. . .oh, no, look who's back off the disabled list!

An: Ah, yes, Marvelous Marbell! And she's got her new laptop protection.

CM: Yep. That's Mary "The Brain" Marbell, last season's most gifted rookie. She has a higher percentage of knowledge than many teachers to begin with, and now with her new equipment. . . .

An: Okay, fans. They're taking their places, and it's almost time for the bell.

CM: Oh, no, Dan, no bells. The bells are broken. Mrs. Close is going to have to get them settled without a bell.

An: No kidding! Isn't the clock broken also?

CM: It is, Frank, but that's normal for matches these days. Close will have a stopwatch, but she doesn't need it. Her instincts for pacing the event and ending up right on the button after 45 minutes are awesome.

An: And here she comes! [In a stage whisper] She hasn't got any books, isn't even going to the desk. This is an amazing opening play! She's moving over to look out the window!

CM: That's a skillful strategy, Frank! They were all set to ignore her, but now they're a little curious, and Dulcey is going to try to block her.

An: And we're off, fans. Dulcey gets out of her seat. She makes an offensive move to the left, toward the window. But now she's moving back to her seat! A *look*—just a *look* from Close—kept her from scoring! Dan, that is an example of *real* experience!

CM: Actually, the "Look" is one of Close's newer plays. For years, Close had depended on her verbal strength, but the "Withering and Disgusted Look" was something she picked up from Anderson, her old teammate over at Boston Latin, who has just been traded to Chicago for two second-round draft picks.

An: She's now resorted to some classic teacher moves. Still hasn't said a word, however. She's writing on the board.

CM: This is classic Close. She doesn't like her voice to dominate in the classroom, and she works well off the blackboard to focus the opposing team. It's pretty hard to resist watching to see what someone is writing. Sometimes she uses a draw play, sketching diagrams or pictures to lure them in.

An: How does she resist all that chatter and movement in the backfield?

CM: Great concentration, Frank. But mostly confidence; confidence is the cornerstone of her defense.

An: You're right. They're quieting down. What did she write?

CM: Ah, this is an old tactic: "Outline for Final Exam." That's a usual starting position late in the season like this, but an effective one. Close really believes in telling them what you want them to know. Watch what she does next. . . .

An: She's passing out lollipops! This is wild. It is something she has been known to do, but never so *early* in the game. What's going on?

CM: It's a silencing device. The kids' mouths are held in check by the candy, and they can't use their strongest defense: extended random conversation!

An: Okay, here we go. Birdie pretends to fumble the lollipop. She signals Close that she wants another one. Close turns to the left and tosses a "Withering Glance" to Birdie. Close is now facing them. I think she's finally going to take a shot. This verbal opening is crucial. Amazing! She has simply asked them to copy down what's on the board!

CM: It's a simple, straightforward kick-off.

An: And it's working. Dulcey picks up her pencil; Birdie is actually writing; Marbell is adjusting her equipment. In the backfield we can see Yolanda crossing her arms and sitting back in her seat.

CM: Yolanda is a tough competitor. I think we're going to see some key defensive moves here.

An: Okay, folks, Close is making an end move around the desk.

CM: Yeah, this is her approach shot, but she doesn't use it as much as some other teachers do.

An: Now she's SITTING ON THE DESK! I'd call that a slam-dunk.

CM: Right, Frank. She's a formidable talent in the forward position.

An: And now, finally, three-and-a-half minutes into the first period, Close may be finally starting to teach them something. No, it's something else. Dan what are we seeing here?

CM: She's turning over the ball to the class, asking them to toss out to her the highlights they remember from the semester.

An: I see Yolanda is putting her head down on the desk. An evasive play, very gutsy. And, of course, now Close calls on Yolanda. Explain this strategy to us, Dan.

CM: It's a direct lob about yesterday's classwork with an extra spin, asking her if she's feeling all right and might need a drink of water. It should not be too hard for anyone to field.

An: Close seems to like to play fair.

CM: Yes, she gives her opponent the benefit of the doubt and creates a humane playing field.

An: Mary Marbell's got her hand up.

CM: This could be trouble. Marbell likes to go one-on-one with Close.

An: Marbell moves in. She asks what possible use Roman History will be to her *in her future life*! This is a brilliant ploy that is going to result in some exciting volleying.

CM: Unless Close calls it out of bounds, of course.

An: Close is not responding. Maybe she needs to call a time out. This could throw off her entire game plan! Folks, Close is not responding! The silence in the arena is palpable. The tension is unbelievable. Dulcey has stopped chewing her gum and has started to dribble. Yolanda's looking up.

CM: A very aggressive play for her.

An: Now Birdie interferes with her offensive laugh! We have about 30 minutes left in the first period, fans. Now Close has deflected Marbell by telling her she has asked a very good question. But she appears to be stalling. Is Close trying to run the clock down, Dan?

CM: It's a little early in the first half to be doing that, Frank. I think she has something else up her sleeve. As I said, Close likes to let her opponents do most of the talking. Then they often make unforced errors.

An: Dan, Close has now stepped up to the plate; she's asking the entire class what they consider the most useful thing they ever learned. Now she retreats to the blackboard, a rather ordinary defensive move, if you ask me. She's making a chart and writing "THINGS LEARNED" over one column and "USEFULNESS" over the other.

CM: I think she is trying to relate the question to their own experience, Dan. It's a risky move.

An: Why is it risky?

CM: Well, Dulcey is outstanding in this particular situation. See? There she goes!

An: Yes! Dulcey's started to tell a story about herself! It's the "Diversionary Anecdote"! Close is about to lose control of the class! They are moving into nonacademic zone defense. The class is clearly protecting its key player here. It's a power play, and even Yolanda is alert! I can't believe this!

CM: I'm shocked, Frank. I'm beginning to think Close may be hurt. I don't think she's going to be able to pull this one out.

An: She's stolen the ball! *Close has stolen the ball!* She's writing Marvelous Marbell's question on the board! She's including it on the outline for the final exam! The class is stunned. The players are furious with Marbell!

CM: This is extraordinary. I'd say the game's over. It's a darn clever play asking them, "What do we know and what good is it?"

An: It's the kind of play no one can really strike out on, Dan.

CM: She's turning the other team's defense into an offensive strategy of her own. This is what comes from knowing every individual on the opposing team extremely well.

An: Wow, Dan, I'm drained. Hands are up everywhere. Why, it looks like the "wave"! The bases are full. She's got them fielding each other's tosses and even writing on their score pads, and she is hardly breaking a sweat. Do you think this was her game plan all along?

CM: Definitely! She wanted to engage them, and she did it in a subtle way; she just slipped through the defensive line and laid one in. You know, you have to do that with a class like this because they don't allow free throws. You have to make all your points from the field.

An: Folks, we need to take a station break and hear from our sponsors. Don't go away. We'll be right back with more action from this extraordinary match-up.

[Camera fades to ETC Logo, and Theme Music replaces voices.]

Brenda Morrow
3rd Grade Teacher
St. Clement's Episcopal Parish School
El Paso, Texas
16 years

For Each one of them I teach

Brenda Morrow

I teach for them. For all of them. For each one of them.

For Rosellen, who came to school two hours late every day and learned her sounds and her math facts on her own because, at 8 years old, she had to be the adult in the family. For Rosellen, who fought against the odds, found her singing voice, her talent for foreign languages, her penchant for acting, her belief in herself—that she can do anything she wants to do. For Rosellen, I teach.

For Rika, who spoke little English after only six months in this country, at first too timid to try, won an Honorable Mention in a citywide poetry contest—in English. For her triumphant smile of accomplishment, I teach.

For Sean, who always knew he could do anything, who had a supportive and loving family, who, now in his second year at a prestigious university, has his eyes set upon a Senate seat or the Oval Office. For Sean, I teach.

For Jerry, who, after his father was brutally murdered, found the classroom the haven of peace and safety that a small boy craves when his childhood has forever been robbed by the wickedness of the world. For Jerry, I teach.

For Isaac, who was in a "real" school for less than three years of his life, the rest of the time spent with countless tutors across the world as his father—his best and only friend—took him to many countries as part of his job in the foreign service. After Issac's father died, he asked me, his 3rd grade teacher and the only one he knew, to share in his graduation from college and in his upcoming wedding. For Isaac, I gratefully teach.

For Michelle and Amy, who worked hard; who struggled with math facts, spelling tests, reading; and who watched their grades very slowly but consistently rise through hours of studying and hard work. Michelle and Amy told each other as they finally set off for their separate colleges, "Remember, just like Mrs. Morrow told us. We can do anything." For Michelle and Amy, I respectfully teach.

For Randy, who stood in the middle of a "train track set up in the North Pole," who dressed as Santa Claus, and who rang a bell to share the new book *The Polar Express* with a captivated audience of fellow 8-year-olds. Randy died years later in a car accident on his way to visit his new university, his promising life extinguished, his magic to live on in those who love him. Because of Randy I will never look at *The Polar Express* without seeing his precious face. And also for John, who challenged every teacher with his intelligence, who challenged himself with finding truth in books and philosophies, who shared with me that he'd found the peace of God's love in his 17th year and a losing battle with leukemia. For Randy and John, both so cherished, I teach.

For Pablo, who faced the reality of becoming an orphan; for Geneva, who had everything going for her but her father's attention; for Leslie, whose mother's death forced her to live with a father who never knew of her existence, nor cared; for Harmony, who clutched the classroom stuffed animal mascot as she went to the doctor to work through the psychological scars of a nightmarish family situation. For all of them, I teach.

For Frank, who successfully battled his addictions in hospitals, who found and hugged me for the notes I sent. For the privilege to aid Frank in winning the greatest fight of his life, I teach.

For Naomi, whose eyes have seen something dark and sinister, whose ears have heard something evil and menacing, whose fears are real and great; for Naomi, who begins to trust enough to seek a hug and loves enough to share a beautiful smile that lights up a room. For Naomi, I teach.

For all of them, for each of them, I teach. I teach for William, who struggled with his brother's drug abuse and subsequent desperate crimes, and fought to conquer his own temptations; or Meredith, who learned her multiplication facts with no help from her alcoholic mother; for Juanito, whose artistic talents wait while he determinedly works in a grocery store to put himself through school. I teach for Maria, a girl from a culture in which only a male child is truly valued, whose weak self-esteem was transformed so that she is now a strong young woman succeeding at a prominent university and helping young girls in the slums of the city. For William, Meredith, Juanito, and Maria, I teach.

To touch each one of them, I proudly teach. To be touched by each one of them, I humbly teach.

For them, I teach.

Douglas DePice
9th–12th Grade Art Teacher
Secaucus High School
Secaucus, New Jersey
23 years

Interdisciplinary Education for Visionary Thinking

Douglas DePice

A BIRD GLIDED PAST A SWAYING tree, which was silhouetted against floating white clouds. This gentle vision seemed also to move within me, touching my heart and inspiring my soul. That gifted moment offered glimpses of eternity, beauty, and truth. I saw it and understood why artists paint, poets write, scientists create, and teachers educate. I was reminded of a line from John Keats, "I am certain of nothing but the holiness of the heart's affections and the truth of the imagination."

Some time after that experience, I began to wonder if it would be possible to teach that kind of self-encounter to my art students. I thought about lessons in awareness that would help them see in a way that would facilitate such heartfelt connections and inspirations within themselves. Further, I hoped to help them expand their comprehension of the relationships among the subjects they study; that is, to see the connections among math, science, English, and art. I felt sure that such lessons would engage the whole student—heart, mind, and soul.

These are some of the ideas and poetic wanderings that sustain and inspire my passion for teaching. Schopenhauer wrote, "The world is my imagination." I think the world is also our classroom, color palette, soul, and friend with an infinite potential for making connections. As social and spiritual beings, the making of connections that are meaningful on many levels is a lifelong process. With each contact, a simultaneous growth of the heart, mind, and soul takes place. It is a growth that is one with visionary thinking.

History is full of examples of dreamers and visionaries who created great connections (friendships) in heartfelt ways: Walt Whitman with a blade of grass, Newton with gravity, da Vinci with water, Thoreau with Walden Pond, Van Gogh with sunflowers, Einstein with light and energy. Indeed, life is a continuous series of connections (friendships) that are happening with ourselves, others, nature, and God. I believe that teaching this holistic attitude toward life would teach students to tap into the vast reservoir of their creativity and nurture the inchoate visionary within each one. I am attempting to build a curriculum that will teach visionary skills.

I have designed a program that unifies the subjects of art, math, English, and science. I call this program "Visual Thinking." Students are learning to see one thing from four points of view: as metaphor (English); as proportion and quantity (math); as matter, ecology, structure (science); and as expressive form (art). This blending of the disciplines is the essence of visionary thinking, and my experience shows that it can be taught in the classroom.

My objectives have dared me to become a bolder, more passionate teacher. I dare to teach my students to be visionaries, cocreators of friendships. I pose questions to my students to stimulate them to relate the subject matter they are studying to the mystery of the soul (self), the beauty of the earth (nature), the brotherhood and sisterhood of men and women (others), and the love of God. An example of the type of nonlogical, problem-finding questions I ask is, "How many trees are there in a leaf?" These almost Zen-like queries help students access the nonlinear, creative parts of their brains. For most, it's a new way of thinking, and for some it helps them see life as an imaginative odyssey, a journey of discovering the continents, constellations, calculus, and mysteries of the soul. In his poem "Song of Myself," Walt Whitman saw all those things in a single blade of grass.

We owe our students nothing less than truth and beauty if we wish to preserve their spirits and have a sane society. The experience of truth and beauty resides in the ability to integrate the intelligence of the heart's affections and the imagining soul with the thinking mind. This enables students to explore the imaginative content of knowledge.

These ideas are the launching pads to the inner spaces of the heart, mind, and soul. These are the spaces where the intelligence of truth, wisdom, and love abide. These are the spaces that are usually neglected in the curriculum but which truly need to be explored and educated.

In each student is the imaginative potential necessary to continue the work of the visionaries that preceded us. I am sure of this.

Yes, the other day I taught my kids to see the flight of a bird as lines in a drawing (art), as the wild orbit of a radical electron (science), as a metaphor of the soul (English), and as the curve of an Archimedes spiral (math). By exploring the imaginative content of knowledge, my students are becoming visionaries. Knowing this inspires and sustains my passion.

A Child Drawing by Douglas DePice

Kathy Marzilli Miraglia
PreK—4th Grade Art Teacher
Friends Academy
North Dartmouth, Massachusetts
16 years

the Reasons for the seasons

Kathy Marzilli Miraglia

THESE ARE FOUR ACRYLIC PAINTINGS PAINTED IN A WATERCOLOR TECHNIQUE. Each portrait represents a student of mine and a season of the school year. I continue in the profession because of the children. They confirm my faith so many times—with a hug, a simple thank you, or just a comment like, "I like art." I celebrate all children in these portraits.

Ronald Newburgh
9th, 11th, and 12th Grade Physics Teacher
The Rivers School
Weston, Massachusetts
11 years

A Shared Approach to Teaching: Education as a Dialogue

Ronald Newburgh

IT IS NOW 11 YEARS SINCE I RETIRED AS a research physicist and began teaching physics. That was in 1987, 28 years after I received my doctorate. I spent almost this entire time at a Department of Defense research laboratory. They were good years devoted to good scientific problems with military importance. I was fortunate enough to have been able to contribute to their solutions. I left with much satisfaction.

What have I learned from my years as a teacher? It goes without saying that teaching high school physics differs from doing research in a government laboratory. The demands are different in that success is measured by a very human meter stick—the success of students—rather than the solution to a problem. I have learned much about children from teaching. I have told my daughter that when I offer advice about my grandchildren, I am speaking as a teacher, not as a parent.

The pleasure of learning more about children was one that I had anticipated. I did not, however, realize how much my students would teach me about physics. I am not talking about what I learned from them about people, about teaching, about myself. No, I am talking specifically about lessons in science, in physics. Thanks to 11 years of listening to my students, I know that my understanding of physics is deeper today than when I began.

Let me give one specific example. When I was at Worcester Academy, I had an exceptional student. (She went on to Harvard and is now working on her doctorate at the University of California at Santa Barbara.) We had been discussing beat frequencies, a phenomenon associated with the interaction of two waves, each with a single frequency. The usual approach to the analysis of beats depends on a sterile mathematical approach using the addition of sinusoidal functions. For a beginning student, the approach offers no physical intuition and is quite opaque.

My student said that she had not understood my explanation. In the accepted tradition of all teachers, I then repeated the explanation, only more slowly. Naturally, she still did not understand. At that point I was compelled to find an alternate way of looking at the problem. Knowing that she was an excellent athlete as well as an excellent student, I sought a description based on sports. I found it in running.

Consider two runners competing on a circular track. One runs faster than the other. If they start together, the faster will lap the slower. Mathematical analysis shows that the condition for lapping is identical to that for beats.

As soon as we went through this analogy, she understood. The analysis depended upon a physical situation, which she knew. She was able to relate it to personal intuition. At the same time my understanding of beats became deeper. First I realized that beats are a frequency phenomenon not a wave phenomenon *per se*. The concept of phase also became much clearer. This I owe to her. I published the analysis in *The Physics Teacher*, where it had a wide audience and was well received.

Since that time there have been numerous similar incidents. They all began with questions from students when I had not succeeded in an explanation. These questions forced me to rethink a physical situation and, if possible, find alternate explanations. The topics have been varied. How does one draw a force diagram? Why is the tension in a massless string uniform? How do two capacitors come to equilibrium? Why is a ray equivalent to a wave of zero wavelength? In answering these questions I have published some dozen papers with, I believe, valuable insights for teaching. I have learned much physics in the process. Teaching, to be effective, must be a dialogue, not a monologue. The reward is that we all learn.

Never Tire of Learning; Never Tire of Teaching

Wei-ling Wu

WHEN I WAS A STUDENT IN CHINA, I was taught that a good student should "never tire of learning," as the great, ancient Chinese master teacher Confucius said. I remember one winter when several students and I stayed after school in an unheated classroom, puzzling over physics problems and jumping around to warm ourselves. After awhile, our physics teacher came and took us into his office. Sitting around a little charcoal fire in a clay bucket, we listened to him explaining the problems. To this day, I can still feel the warmth from that little charcoal fire and from my teacher.

> 學而不厭，
> 誨人不倦。
> 孔子《論語》
>
> Never tire of learning;
> Never tire of teaching.
>
> THE ANALECTS, CONFUCIUS

When I was a young teacher, I was challenged by Confucius's words, "never tire of teaching." The memory of the little fire lit by my teacher inspired me to love my students and to light little fires in their hearts. However, at that time, I did not really know how, except for that sincere love in my heart.

Since then, I have been called "my teacher" by students from 1st grade to graduate school, and I have taught in China and America, where the educational systems are worlds apart. Now, with 30 years of teaching experience, I have a better understanding of the way Confucius lit fires in his students' hearts: When he was very determined to do something, he forgot about eating; when he was very happy, he forgot about being sad; when he was very determined and very happy, he forgot about getting old.

Determination is the driving force of passion. Spiritual reward is the fountain for enthusiasm. My students have given me determination and boundless spiritual rewards. There was a Chinese boy in a middle school English class I taught in China. For two years, when I opened the door of my apartment in Shanghai on the morning of the first Chinese New Year's Day, he would be standing there with a little cake in his hand. He wanted to be the first one to say "Happy New Year" to the teacher he loved and respected. American students demonstrate their love in different ways: thank-you cards; warm words; big hugs; and, most preciously, their love for the Chinese culture and their perseverance in learning Chinese. Looking at these students singing, dancing, and speaking Chinese, that little fire in my heart lit by my teacher has become an inferno. I feel I have unlimited energy and enthusiasm that enable me to imagine, to be innovative, and to be determined to make changes in my teaching.

> 發憤忘食，
> 樂以忘憂，
> 不知老之將至云爾！
>
> When one is very determined,
> One forgets about eating;
> When one is very happy,
> One forgets about being sad;
> When one is very determined and very happy,
> One forgets about getting old.
>
> THE ANALECTS, CONFUCIUS

Indeed, we learn; we teach; we forget about "food," "worries," and "old age." We have boundless joy and tremendous passion for being teachers.

Wei-ling Wu
9th–12th Grade Teacher of Chinese
West Windsor–Plainsboro High School
Princeton Junction, New Jersey
30 years

Pamela M. Morgan
6th–9th Grade Learning Strategist
Renbrook School
West Hartford, Connecticut
27 years

Scenes from a Teaching Life

Pamela M. Morgan

Scene 1: Encountering

In 1970 she arrived at her first job at a peculiar hybrid boarding and local high school in the Northeast Kingdom of Vermont. She arrived knowing everything about Spanish verb tenses and Latin American magical realism and nothing about teenagers and teaching. She was to be the Spanish department, intended to be the prophet of a new, rigorous curriculum after years of a mutually and benignly apathetic arrangement between an aging alcoholic gentleman and his many unengaged charges.

She planned to rescue and ignite in them a love of the sounds and codes of the language through a study of guerilla poetry from Colombia, written by soldiers not much older than themselves. They balked; they came empty-handed and empty-headed to class; they made fun of the patriotism and martyrdom in translation. She despaired and gave them quizzes on the imperfect tense.

One day in the spring, a shy back-row girl with a dangerous interest in hallucinogens and truancy inexplicably came to her and recited this poetry:

> "Yo no me río   No, I don't laugh
> de la muerte.   at death.
> Sucede simplemente,   It's just that
> que no tengo miedo   I'm not afraid
> de morir entre   to die among
> pájaros y árboles. . . ."   birds and trees. . . .

"I like that, señora."

Scene 2: Discovering

In 1971 she moved to southern Vermont with her new husband, who was studying for a master's degree in education. She took the only job open to her, a state-funded assistant teacher/school secretary position in a three-room schoolhouse on the dark side of Stratton Mountain.

The daily 50-mile commute over winding, climbing, plunging, icy roads was nothing compared to reading time with Billy John.

Robert Brown, as his records explained, was 1 of 23 first and second cousins enrolled in that 57-student school. At age 7, he knew all about snowmobiles but nothing about toothbrushes. He could not wait to be old enough to miss school days for the fall hunting season. He didn't ever expect to be able to read a book. He had little patience for the young teacher assigned to help him sound out incomprehensible marks on a paper.

Nothing worked. Bobby had no interest in drawing, singing, chanting, or decoding by color. The year was limping by. And then, one day, he brought a sprig of bittersweet to school. Barely able to speak in his excitement, he pointed out the tightly paired sets of scarlet berries to the mystified assistant teacher and taught her an astounding lesson: "The berries look like the first letter in both my names, and they sound the same, too!"

Scene 3: Listening

The scene changed and the teaching couple, he with a new degree in education and she with teaching in her blood, moved to a Connecticut girls boarding school to become house directors, teachers, advisors, coaches.

Because there were no Spanish sections in need of a newcomer, she filled her hours listening and advising, seldom mindful of the fact that she was only five years older than some of her advisees.

She heard that the schoolwork was hard for the girls, many of whom battled the chronic sadness of being away from families and familiar routines. Such a girl was Myra. She could not describe her misery, but it was evident to her advisor. She was determined to do everything right, and her soft Nashville accent carried tales of attempts and failures, near successes, and mysteries. She could not speak in class; she wanted to. She was not tapped for Glee Club; she loved to sing. Her parents waited for joyful tales at the other end of the phone line; she made things up.

Her advisor listened, ached, and reassured, "It will get better. Surely your teachers see how hard you are trying. Talk to them. Be straight with your parents."

Myra came often to her advisor's apartment to talk. Her advisor listened. In January, Myra left school under a cloud when a set of history tests crucial for determining term grades was found secreted under her bedsprings. There was no time for more questions and reassurances, but her tearful advisor vowed to listen better to the next Myra who came along.

Scene 4: Sensing and Studying

After a time, her own children were born and she moved to a day school where they could all learn and teach together. Her youngest Spanish students, 1st and 3rd graders, were willing to suspend their grip on English when she was with them. They loved the sound of the new words and the game of decoding. Some who struggled with the tasks of reading or writing in English were set free to tell stories or rhymes, relying on the vivid memories of sounds and actions. Their teachers were stunned when these "at-risk" students put on plays or held conversations in Spanish.

The group of young students who most occupied her thoughts and influenced her planning were the "nudges," the ones who wandered off, both literally and figuratively, in class, the ones who blurted out answers or funny comments and never had the right "stuff" or the right page. Her son was one of them.

Her own painful education began when her son's 1st grade teacher suggested an attention deficit disorder. There was a name for these energetic, adorable, confounding mavericks, after all. She read unceasingly and indiscriminately, attended workshops, forced herself not to proselytize about the condition. She transformed herself into a combination Spanish teacher and "learning strategist."

It was not easy to hold on to her new understandings. Some days her colleagues and husband almost convinced her that she was preoccupied with merely naughty or over-indulged children, including her own son, who were bent on sabotaging her classes. She had to believe, though, that these children were prisoners of their own inabilities to choose and hold on to the appropriate behavior or thought for the moment. She continued to rehearse and debrief situations with her Attention Deficit Disorder kids; she commiserated with fellow parents and exhorted them to be open and objective about the inevitable ups and downs of their children's school careers. She convinced her family and herself over time.

Ten years after she undertook the low-key campaign to learn and to teach about differences in learning and attention, a veteran teacher from the upper school history department came to her for the first time to ask about managing Attention Deficit Disorder in her classroom. She explained that she had heard other teachers talking in the faculty room about a difficult student they shared. She heard that they had gotten some clues for helping this student to succeed from the "learning strategist." She wanted to know what this was all about.

Scene 5: Graduating

Not getting any younger, but still exhilarated by the collision of the worlds of children and ideas, she steeled herself to go back to school. In 1992 she was one of three "gringas" in a class of 25 Cuban, Puerto Rican, and Dominican teachers. She signed a contract agreeing to speak only Spanish for every waking hour of five summer weeks and to write a chapter in Spanish for a resource book on ways to use authentic materials from the islands in elementary Spanish classes. The effort of entering other cultures, making sense of them, not giving offense, and staying with the pace of the talk made her nauseous at times. She almost gave up, twice.

But when she danced the Merengue at a club in Washington Heights for her graduation party and when she engineered an exchange program between her 4th graders and those at the Ramon Betances School, she knew that she had gotten to a new place. And there would always be new places.

Beth Spencer
4th Grade Teacher
Roosevelt School
Neenah, Wisconsin
23 years

I Love Teaching so Much that I Quit

Beth Spencer

I LOVE TEACHING SO MUCH THAT I quit. Twice, in fact. In 1986, after teaching in several elementary schools for almost 12 years, I left the role of classroom teacher for that of elementary guidance counselor. It was from this position that I began to gain new perspectives on being a teacher.

Leaving the classroom gave me fresh insights into three crucial areas: parents, administrators, and teachers. In the counselor role, I had more intimate contacts with parents than I had when teaching. I developed deeper understandings of the issues parents struggle with set within the context of wide family issues, like alcoholism, poverty, abuse, and grief. I developed increased respect for their efforts and strengthened my belief that nothing of positive value is gained for children by devaluing their parents. Through the choices and attitudes they expressed, the parents of the students I counseled frequently manifested a lack of appropriate parenting in their own childhoods, and I learned that any support I could offer the parent would benefit the child. The many home visits I undertook reinforced a growing conviction that even the seemingly least effective parents are often trying hard to do their best within the limits of their understanding and experience. The walls of the poorest houses displayed their children's school pictures, and *their* refrigerators, too, blossomed with their children's drawings. An abiding love was apparent.

Some families taught their children to fear outsiders in an effort to protect them from a prying and threatening world. Inadvertently, perhaps, the children also learned a kind of shame, a sense that they were also not good enough. Some administrators with whom I worked instilled in their teachers this sort of exaggerated self-protection. In an era of "teacher bashing" there is, perhaps, a tendency to close in, to circle the wagons, to create an ethic of caution. Working as a counselor, however, I found that strategy stifling and nonproductive. More and more I grew to believe in parents as partners.

I also despaired of an attitude toward children that felt negative and punitive, designed to create barriers rather than bridges. I became convinced that both children and adults could be helped to develop more socially cooperative behaviors by using techniques that *reframed* their behaviors and their motives in positive ways. Learning and using the language of mediation was also very helpful as I sought to help children and families compromise and resolve conflicts. While both of these techniques are grounded in respect for individuals, they strengthen affiliations among people.

Working as a specialist gave me opportunities to observe many more classrooms and teachers than I could as a classroom teacher. I learned much in the way of specific and effective teaching strategies from my colleagues' examples. But I also learned to value my own good teaching. I learned that other teachers also struggle with curriculum, parents, classroom management, finding time enough, and with meeting all those divergent needs. I found no magic teacher in a flawless classroom where all children learned optimally. I found I was "enough."

In 1993, I was once again a quitter. This time, I undertook the risky adventure of a year of unpaid leave for no "good" reason. I wasn't pregnant, wasn't sick, wasn't even all that tired. I just knew that this was what I needed to do. I also knew that I would be assigned to an undetermined classroom position on my return to my district. But, with the encouragement of an unbelievably supportive husband, I was able to follow my heart into some truly enriching experiences. During that time, I worked as a volunteer in a national park, traveled out of the country for the first time, swam with pink dolphins in the Amazon, rafted the San Juan River, sat for eight silent days in meditation, read, wrote, and dreamed. I was able to focus on an amazing journey within my own soul, a journey that fed me well then and nurtures me still. And I gained so much to share with my students.

Back in a classroom now, I model risk-taking, adventuring, foolishness: possibility. I am less afraid to hug, to laugh, to sing out loud. Koshare, the sacred clown of the Hopi, is my patron saint. I am still committed to accountability, to time-on-task, to excellence, but I now know that *I* am the most influential presence in the classroom, not textbooks or curriculum. The children listen to my *life*, not just my lesson plans. It is an honor, a privilege, and a great responsibility to teach. So go ahead and quit! You'll be back, and you'll love it even more!

Patricia Hall Curvin
12th Grade English Teacher
English Chair
Arts High School
Newark, New Jersey
20 years

Old-fashioned Values Meet New-fashioned Young Adults

Patricia Hall Curvin

TO RETURN TO TEACHING 11 YEARS ago, I had to have my eyes wide open. Teaching in urban America means less prestige, inadequate compensation, antiquated buildings, and students who can read but have not read much. I had held administrative positions at Educational Testing Service and Rutgers University. Both offered status, staff, and comfortable surroundings. So why return? It was my passion for teaching.

My story is a tale of old-fashioned values meet new-fashioned young adults. I have had to be prepared to teach 15- and 17-year-olds, both professionally and physically. Good health and stamina, as well as consistent academic planning, are indispensable to a teacher's success.

I returned to teach in Newark, New Jersey—a city that has only recently begun to "turn itself around." The school system is comprised of 82 schools and 50,000 students. Three years ago, the district was taken over by the state because of inept management and gross inefficiencies. However, I teach at a magnet school for the arts known as Arts High School. It is a school founded in the 1930s that singer Sarah Vaughn attended decades ago and, most recently, graduated dancer Savion Glover. Arts High School now serves 550 students, whose talents range from instrumental and vocal music to drama, dance, and fine arts. These "right brainers" are visually capable and, like other teenagers across America, would rather not read.

With the participation of students, my classroom is brought to life with plants, posters, lights, and a colorful rug that serves as the room's "stage." The desk is simply a piece of furniture, not a barrier between me and students. Nor is it a resting place; I pace the aisles. At the door, I greet my kids and begin teaching at the bell. Pace, movement, and involvement for every moment of the 42 teaching minutes get us through difficult lessons, unpopular work, but challenging experiences.

Perhaps my students have found me to be an anomaly. I address them as "Miss" or "Mr." I dress formally. Rarely am I absent; I am totally engaged in my lessons. And I do not mind calling parents. Though it is *my* classroom, students have found their voices through writing and speaking assignments. They are loud, energetic, funny, clever, and, once they get going, they want to learn and to succeed. My expectations are high—not unreasonable, but constant. I annoy them with civilities: no gum-chewing; pass it, don't throw it; "shut up" is simply banned.

Learning new ideas and approaches makes teaching even more fun. In the last few years, for example, I supervised a student teacher who was terrific at using projects. Colleagues in music, dance, and theater have helped me fine-tune both my approaches to my literature and to my students. I encourage students to use their artistic interests, which got them to Arts High in the first place, and to learn about classical literature. Let me give you some examples of what one class produced when we studied *A Separate Peace* by John Knowles. Knowles sets his coming-of-age novel during World War II. In depicting this era, students produced a broad range of projects:

- Original World War II propaganda posters
- A dance routine for "The Bugle Boy Blues"
- Letters to soldiers' mothers and sweethearts
- A chronicle of war in collage form
- A jazz trio playing Duke Ellington and songs of Ella Fitzgerald
- Original animated videos
- A 1940s fashion show

At the conclusion of a four-day extravaganza of performance and exhibition, we recapped the novel and wondered if any of the characters ever listened to the music on the radio or passed by such posters supporting the war.

Whether it's the 1960s or the '90s, students remain the reason—not the literature—for walking into a classroom. These adolescents can make me laugh and cry. Their energy can consume the classroom. Though every day is not special, many days include exploration, discovery, and even joy. The students embody the promise of things to come, and my engagement with them links me to their future as well as my own.

Benjamin H. Thomas
9th–12th Grade Social Studies Teacher
Thornton Friends School
Silver Spring, Maryland
33 years

Ten Experiences in Which Somebody Learned Something

Benjamin H. Thomas

1. All of the camping trips, but the lousy-weather ones most of all.

2. All of the times that the kids were too busy to notice that I was down the hall getting a cup of coffee.

3. Most of the times when I proposed an assignment and a kid would say, "Why can't we do _____ instead?"

4. One-third of the times when I didn't know what I was going to do when I walked into the room. (All of the times when I didn't know what I was going to do and admitted it to myself, and maybe to the students.)

5. The time when we finished a unit on railroads and the kids said, "We've learned too much to stop here." So we built a museum in the basement.

6. The times when I was working with baffling kids, never knowing what I was doing, and never doing it right, except that at the end of the year some of those kids were in great shape.

7. All of the times that we were all laughing.

8. The time that I cried in the bathroom because I couldn't save a kid no matter how much I loved him.

9. The time I ran into a former 8th grade, major thorn-in-my-side student who said he was now teaching middle school. (I said, "That almost makes me believe in revenge—but I'm not sure which way.")

10. The times I was patient and powerless.

The Power of Words

Harry E. Wilson, Jr.
K–12th Grade Director of Art Education
Summit Public Schools
Summit, New Jersey
29 years

I Teach

Harry E. Wilson, Jr.

I learn so I may teach

I teach because I learn

I teach because it's hard

I teach because it's easy

I teach to share the treasures I have found

I teach to show how one may find one's own treasures

I teach to see more clearly

I teach for the joy of watching children learn

I teach to see them thrive from knowledge

I teach to see children sharing, discovering, teaching. . .learning

I teach to share the joy of learning

I teach to see the smiles

I teach to smile

    I smile often

Works of Change

Harry E. Wilson, Jr.

mixed media, 1996

Hamilton Salsich
Middle School English Teacher
Pine Point School
Stonington, Connecticut
25 years

Living Well in the Classroom

Hamilton Salsich

THE OTHER DAY, ONE OF MY 9TH GRADE students stopped after class and asked why I enjoyed teaching so much. She tossed the question to me, like you would toss a ball to someone. I think I answered, "Because it's fun." But at home that night, clearer, deeper answers came.

Thirty years ago, I chose teaching as a career for one reason: Certain books had changed my life, and I wanted to help make that happen for others. I had discovered Ralph Ellison's *Invisible Man* one September night, reading aloud whole chapters in my college room, sometimes shouting in amazement or sorrow. On another night, I had stayed up late with the puzzling, spirited poems of Emily Dickinson, saying them over and over to myself, hearing phrases that sounded like songs made just for me. During a year's residence in New Hampshire, I had read both *The Iliad* and *War and Peace*, and I remember feeling as I was reading that the boundaries of my life were shifting in irrevocable ways.

For me the power of books has always had much to do with *seeing*. When I read words set down with grace and strength, I seem to see life more sharply. Simple things start shining again, as they should. It's like cleaning my glasses or studying leaves with a hand lens: Through reading, a few things in life can come suddenly, marvelously, into focus.

And is there anything we need more in our world than the ability to see clearly what's happening around us? Is there anything more menacing than the blindness that seems so widespread today—the blindness that allows politicians to steal from constituents and husbands to hurt wives and so many of us to disregard the cries of the afflicted? This is a blindness that seals not only eyes but souls.

At times each of us succumbs to this beguiling blindness, which is why literature has been so essential to humankind and continues to be essential to me and my students. A story about suffering has helped us see and understand suffering, and poems about valor have helped us know and cherish valor. When we read well, we open our eyes and the universe is once again startling. In an important sense, when we read well, we *live* well.

And after all, isn't living well what education is or should be all about? Shouldn't I, as a teacher, ultimately want to help my students live a little more thoroughly, a little more ardently? In this sense, being a teacher is a lofty honor and carries with it substantial responsibilities. A teacher must be the kind of person John Dewey described when he distinguished between a mere *trainer* and a genuine *teacher*. A trainer simply wants to help the students perform certain tasks; a teacher wants to help the students *alter their lives*. I, for one, have no interest in being a trainer. I want to help my students feel the emancipation that comes from the patient study of inspired books—the feeling of being free to live, right now, this moment, with more poise and spirit. I believe that's my job as an English teacher. I see myself as a freedom fighter for my students' right to cherish and take delight in this sublime universe; my weapons are poems, stories, plays, and essays.

My students, though, must toil for their own emancipation. Our young people need no further coddling. They need teachers who demand instead of plead, push instead of pamper. They need English teachers who think theirs is a grand calling and who are not afraid to announce to their students that in this class works of immense strength will be read, works which have the power to break up the frozen sea inside you and force the scales to fall from your eyes so that you see with a new precision. Words of wisdom and vision will be read every day, and you will have to labor diligently in the pages of books so that the wisdom and vision will come to you and stay with you. There will be no shortcuts, no high-interest abridgments, no *Cliff's Notes*, no "drugstore-novels-because-at-least-they'll-be-reading" units. There will simply be words and sentences containing dangerous explosives, and I, your teacher, will do my best to ignite them.

Yesterday I tossed the ball back to my student. I told her I am proud and grateful to be a teacher, especially an English teacher. I said I love being shocked and stirred by great works of literature, and I love helping my students feel the kind of awe I feel when I read words written splendidly. I told her I wish to live well with my students, reaching and rising and blossoming and raising our voices in wonder, book after book.

Elizabeth June Wells
9th—12th Grade English Teacher
St. Martin's Episcopal School
Metairie, Louisiana
35 years

Chasing Words in the Classroom

Elizabeth June Wells

I LOVE CHASING WORDS. THEY WRITHE and wriggle and defy me to pin them down on the page. And when I think I have won and can afford to collapse in bed, I wake up to discover that in the night those words have crawled off and left only my sweat smeared on the page.

In my English and Creative Writing classes I like to see my students stare at empty air as they chase words around my classroom. As advisor to the literary magazine, I work for the day when a student sees her own short story in print or another loses his breath when a classmate's poem speaks directly to him.

One of my students wrote, "A poet is a madman whispering on a street corner."* He may be right in that inspired verses do not depend on an acoustically designed hall. But my student-poets are offering important pieces of their world to those who will listen. Too often, in the drive to improve Advanced Placement scores, the honest voices of our young people are buried in the language of expository analysis, their intuitive leaps ignored as lucky guesses. In our workshop sessions my fellow writers and I have learned to listen to painful realities like "killing is not a difficult skill to learn." But the sounds of "jealous leaves that sigh and flex before beauty and desire" are so seductive that we forget to analyze the image.

My students' words encourage me to know their stories, to relive a childhood rejection when "my heart crushed, like a crisp cracker, crumbling in my hand." Their poems can plunge me into their uncertain worlds where "darkness lurks inside my head like a dusty road." With them, I feel the terror that "crawls deep in my throat as the empty house swallows me," or know the dull void inside when love fails and "feelings are faded like a ruined painting."

Sometimes my students take me where I do not want to go. They drag me into the despair of the old man in the rest home who cries out, "Who am I but an ancient clown nibbling a melon, a tissue scarecrow hunched over checkers." Other times, they unknowingly lay healing hands on my most persistent anxieties. Last year, as I carefully hugged my mother, who seemed to grow smaller as I held her, I heard a student's poem to his mother:

> The eternal vertebrae
> Each meticulously supporting the next
> You are the cushion that turns
> Jagged edges of danger
> Into rose petals of sweet softness

In struggling with language, we create ourselves and our world. As long as my students and I keep language alive and honest, teaching will be worth the struggle. When the third cup of coffee hasn't kicked in yet, lunch duty looms, and my orthopedic supports feel like rocks, I can still walk with the step of a freshman teacher because my students seem always ready to "sing the words to songs we've never heard, drink the morning's juice and just revel in being alive."

*All student quotations have appeared in St. Martin's Episcopal School's art and literary magazine, *The Lyre*.

Reflections

Katharine L. Philip
9th–12th Grade Art Teacher
Leonia High School
Leonia, New Jersey
16 years

Women and Tools

Katharine L. Philip

When our high school wood shop closed, the used tools found a home in our art room. I asked my students to draw them and was stunned by their innovative and beautiful drawings. Their work inspired me to create a series of works that combine and contrast the mechanical forms of tools with humanity as depicted by the female form.

Ultimately, the human form, both in mind and body, is a marvelous tool. We are instruments constructing our destiny as surely as tools create our physical environment.

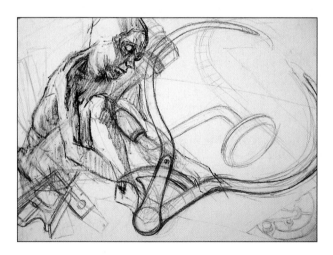

orbitals

Katharine L. Philip

The circular elliptical paths traversed by spacecraft, satellites, planets, or other heavenly bodies inspire these works. The orbital path of a planet is a balance between the gravitational pull of a larger body and the propulsion, the forward motion, of the smaller object. The periodic revolution of a planet is similar to the balancing act people perform as they negotiate their lives. We revolve around what is important to us (ambitions, love, ideas, religion, work) in an effort to find an orbital path of equilibrium to sustain us. These works aspire to combine the cosmic and the mundane.

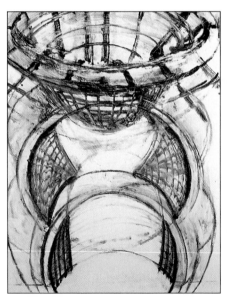 

My Biological Clock Is Ticking

Katharine L. Philip

This monotype aims to draw an analogy between the round, fruitful pendulum shape and the unpregnant female. She is hanging on to the pendulum, perhaps because time is sliding by quickly, or perhaps in a futile effort to slow it down. Below the woman dangles sperm-man with his key to the clock. Apparently, a man has less trouble with time. I hope that I imbued the man with a quiet air of dignity, self-satisfaction, and interest. His ability to father a child is overshadowed by the woman's monthly cycles. He has the key, but she has the clock, so they hang together.

Peter E. Murphy
9th–12th Grade English Teacher
Atlantic City High School
Atlantic City, New Jersey
21 years

Still Life with Mothers

Peter E. Murphy

Hope is Not a Method is the title of a film on birth
control I planned to show my class of teenaged mothers,
but was daunted by the requests from their own under thirty
moms, the grand mothers and daughters of poverty's hunger,
that they too desired to sit in on the viewing.
The room is alive with the cracking of gum as light
scatters across the glittering screen that hangs willy-nilly
from the cracked green wall painted last fifteen years ago.
The sound track snaps alive mid-sentence as light breaks
into chunks, floats invisibly in the dark orbit until it splotches
on the screen which sparkles with the attention of the mothers
who nod, who chuckle, who say, You got that right, Girl! conversing
with the film, laughing when the demonstrator rolls a condom
over a banana, which cracks everyone up, even me.
The room fills with Can you imagine? and That ain't nothing!
and I wonder if she's gonna eat it?

When the film ends and the students and their mothers rise,
the world seems almost over. It is February, a three-window day,
all open to cool the room stifled by the valve-broken radiator.
I wish I could turn it off, I apologize to no one in particular.
It ain't your fault, Honey, a grandmother says. You do what you can.

And they thank me for letting them come to school as the bell rings

us into a passing period when the hallways fill with noise

and fights and locker lovers who make out between science and art.

They leave me to rewind the film in the dark, rolling

the celluloid links over the small sprockets, making it

all race backwards, making sure I'll be ready in four minutes

when the next class enters, making sure my grade book is open,

my seating chart correct, my lesson plans up to date.

Then I will call out their names.

I will blaze for forty-two minutes, and later, I will wrap

my arms around my own teenaged daughter.

I will love my wife.

I will lie sleepless in bed counting the faces of the dead.

I will teach myself to hope.

Polishing

Jane Sprouse

I was too young, of course—
aren't we all?—
to know what I was in for.

That first June, worn
to a nub of my former, invincible self,
I gave it one more year.

Twenty-seven Junes now, have worn
the edges, smoothed
the flaws,

polished
the rough stone
I was.

But the lustrous sheen
is deceptive.
I am

all too aware
of the fissures below
the surface.

Remember me?

Jane Sprouse

On cold nights,
I can warm myself by the fire
of the serious Alfonzo,
who finally learned to read.

The tooth-sharp memory of a tough and rangy tomboy
crying beneath
that spindly sapling, afraid to go home,
lies waiting in a crooked smile.

Blond girls in anachronistic uniforms
dance through my dreams, holding the walnut stained hands
of the children of migrant workers.
If I wanted to forget, I could not.

They come back to visit now,
on the doorstep with voices
like kettle drums.
"Do you remember me?" they ask.

They do not know
what has been voiced
is the secret, shameful question
of teachers.

Jane Sprouse
K–8th Grade Learning Specialist
Katherine Delmar Burke School
San Francisco, California
27 years

Kathy Prout
K—8th Grade Teacher
Coordinator of Gifted and Talented Programs
Frank Antonides School
West Long Branch, New Jersey
29 years

Sent to Siberia

Kathy Prout

OKAY, I ADMIT IT. BECAUSE OF THE way I taught, I was sent to Siberia. I returned home only to be sent back again three years later. I know what you are thinking, but this was no banishment. The image that many have of icy Siberian wastelands where recalcitrants are sent to rethink their former ways is not the place that I have come to know. But then, my presence there was due to an award, not a punishment, an award that I could only receive because I am a teacher.

In 1994 I received a grant from the International Crane Foundation to travel with a group of educators to an area of Far East Russia where endangered cranes nest each summer. Our task was to help set up educational programs for local villagers to consider together the value of nearby wetland nesting grounds, which are easily destroyed by local farming practices. U.S. agricultural experts were on hand to share information with farmers on new techniques that would be less destructive to the wetlands and more agriculturally productive.

Although I spent months preparing for this experience, I arrived without a notion of the deep fondness and friendships that would grow in just a few weeks between the warm Siberian villagers and me. In fact, I had been disappointed when I first realized that participating in this program would keep me from having a personal half-century celebration with friends and family on my July 4 birthday. How could I have known that my new Russian friends would not dream of letting such an occasion pass without serious celebration?

In place of the traditional 4th-of-July fireworks and American birthday festivities, I was treated to one surprise after another, each highlighting in a unique way the thoughtfulness, talent, and ingenuity of our Russian hosts. On the morning of my 50th birthday, we heard a particular bird, the buttonquail, sing for us for the first time. Our host ornithologist announced that it was singing for my birthday. He went on to explain that only the female sings and that she does so to attract males. When she is successful, she mates with them, deposits her eggs in several nests, and flies off, leaving the males to care for the young. I wondered if there were a metaphor in this tale that I should take to heart.

On July 4, we traveled to the village of Arkara to visit their federally funded School for Art and Music. We were told that the children would perform for us, but we never expected the stunning talent they displayed. Diminutive dancers breezed across the stage in colorful wildflower costumes. The children's ballet performances and pieces performed on flute, piano, and accordion were exquisite. In the midst of these talented performances an announcement was made in Russian, and the music teacher leapt onto the stage to play "Happy Birthday" on the piano. I wondered at my good fortune to be in this place on my birthday with such caring and creative people.

Later that evening, called from my tent to dinner, I put away my journal and hurried to the two-story cabin where we had our meals at the Khinganski Nature Reserve. I entered the cabin to Russian-accented shouts of "Surprise!" The mayor of a local village escorted me to a birthday "throne," decorated with feathers donated by molting cranes. Lena, the camp cook, had secretly baked and decorated a birthday cake, which she presented to me along with five wildflowers, one for each decade of my life. Through an interpreter, she told me that the flowers were a special gift, "woman to woman." Throughout dinner we, of course, had the customary toasts with vodka and champagne, which loosened up our vocal chords for the hours of singing and laughter around a campfire that followed. What a memorable birthday it was!

A few days and many bumpy roads later, we arrived at Muraviovka Nature Reserve for the opening ceremony of the environmental camp we were helping to initiate. The delightful Russian children who would be attending our camp gave a performance that stole the show. Dressed as storks, cranes, and poachers, they vividly portrayed the problems facing wild birds in their wetlands. It set the scene for all of the creativity and exuberance the children would exhibit as we worked with them in the week to follow.

I couldn't wait to share my experiences with my students and to bring Russia and its people alive for them through personal accounts, slides, and mementos. I had brought photos and letters with me from my students, who were hoping for Russian penpals. I was thrilled when 35 of my students began a correspondence with children I had met at Muraviovka. They exchanged letters, photos, and small gifts. They made a personal connection, which for so many years had not been possible between Russians and Americans.

Then we got some really wonderful and unexpected news. Three of the most creative and talented Russian teachers involved in the project had received a grant to visit the United States and would visit our schools and communities the following spring. Several parents of my students chose to be present when the Russian teachers visited my classroom. My student, Kristen, had been corresponding with Katia, the daughter of one of the visiting teachers. At the moment that Kristen's mother and Katia's mother saw each other in person for the first time, tears formed in both women's eyes, and they embraced as if they were long-lost relatives. It is a memory I will always cherish as one of the most profoundly moving experiences of my teaching career.

I am a sponge that literally cannot contain all of the experiences that I soak up in my travels, so I spill them out in my classroom. Posters, photographs, artifacts, toys, clothing, and books help me share my experiences with my students, and others in my school and community. I often feel like a traveling cultural exhibit and count myself fortunate to have such opportunities to make the world feel accessible and familiar to young people.

Knowing I will be sharing my experiences with students helps me to see more deeply when I travel. With every photograph I take, I am mindful that my camera will enable me to carry a whole country around in a slide carousel. Every year, my summer experiences are incorporated into the curriculum I teach. This year, my students and Russian children made a new connection when they had their artwork and writing about endangered cranes published together in a special issue of a children's international publication called *The Wild Times*.

The Russian project I have described is the most recent of many summer experiences I have had since 1986, which have kept my teaching spirit alive. In addition to my Russian travels, I have explored Costa Rica, Malaysia, Australia, and Israel on teacher fellowships. I have studied everything from howler monkeys to Leonardo da Vinci and the Renaissance to the mythological works of Ovid and Virgil.

Summer is the time to have the experiences that will add spice to your teaching. Each of my summer experiences has greatly influenced my teaching. Whatever your field or grade level, grants and fellowships await you for summer professional growth. Go for it!

Don't Waste the Day

Okey Canfield Chenoweth

Don't waste the day
thinking about the night
though the coming guests
be unbearably exciting,
though they light up all
your trees, though they
ring all your bells,
though they re-pave
main street and line it
with litter buckets,
though they pave it with
gold and pipe in
angel rock or saints'
songs. The night
will come and with
it stars—but you will
have missed the dawn,
flowers on the lawn,
the mailman,
epiphanies of solitude,
grass green as love,
snow slides, wind
falls, vapors rising,
absolute frost, ultimate
ice, and tumbling
sun bathers that allow
oceans to touch them
where people never can.

Okey Canfield Chenoweth
9th–12th Grade Drama and English Teacher
Glen Rock High School
Glen Rock, New Jersey
42 years

What About You?

Okey Canfield Chenoweth

A THOUSAND YEARS AGO (1935), I walked through the meadow by the stacks of new-mown hay into a one-room country school in West Virginia. The summer corn had been hoed and was ripening in the field. Soon the frost would come and cover the oaks and maples and the new-mown grass, and in October the snow would begin to fly and come to rest on the rows of young pines growing against the hill outside my window at school.

Inside, an iron pot-bellied stove stood in the middle of the room. On a really cold day, the stove would give off not only heat but light as the lower bowl of the stove turned red. On either side of the stove sat about 30 kids, ages 6 through 14 and grades 1 through 8, their faces, arms, legs, and feet tan or brown from the summer sun of corn fields and harvest. At the end of the room was the teacher, a potential source of warmth and light.

On the first day of school calm anticipation filled the room. What do people do all day with no cows to milk, no corn to hoe, and no hay to put up? What a marvelous phenomenon—the freshest part of the day set aside for learning. School seemed almost magical on that long-ago September morning. More than a half century later, the same opportunity to learn and create seems no less wonderful.

For many years, I have had the opportunity to work with and observe high school students as they learned their lessons, played their hearts out on the courts and fields, and acted their hearts out on the stage. As a teacher of English, speech, and drama, I also have had the good fortune to work with students as they discovered some of the great literature and looked for the paths to finding and expressing their own authentic selves through actions and words.

As a child, I loved the huge word "remarkable" when I found it in my first reader. Soon I discovered that words themselves were remarkable—small, naked words in magic combination. Shakespeare's "To be, or not to be. . ." inspired me. The words "from whose bourn no traveler returns. . ." were clothed in mystery and dread. "Howl, howl, howl, howl! Oh you are men of stones/Had I your tongues and eyes I'd use them so/that heaven's vault should crack" shook me to the depths of my being and carried me to the edge of our kinship with other creatures that cry in the night. Words also carry us across cultures and through time to express the feelings of the first people as they came down from the trees and emerged from the caves, fighting off other creatures with sticks of fire. Words carry us across to other species—from the eye of the iris to the wings of the hummingbird.

Each summer of my childhood I would look forward to the words of the new books my teachers would bring me from the county library. I would look forward to seeing my teachers again, many of whom were kind, some of whom were quite nurturing. A few had stolen fire from the gods!

One above all the rest was Claire Wickersham Fiorentino, my college drama teacher. She had an aura of magic and mystery; she seemed to be in touch with extraordinary powers of this world and beyond. From the perspective of a half century later, I think simply that she was in touch with her deepest self and had acquired extraordinary powers of self-expression. On first meeting her, I sensed that she had the power to start me on my own long path of self-discovery and self-expression. Mrs. "F," as we learned to call her, became my lifelong mentor, spiritual mother, and friend. She was perhaps the most fully realized human being I have ever had as a friend. She is gone now, but, on occasion, dressed in black, wearing a single strand of pearls and wagging her finger gently, she still directs me in dreams. "You must do this, do that, Okey, or the world will never know!"

At first Mrs. "F" and I eyed each other warily. I had reason to believe she thought I was hopeless. "He's very smart but the most undramatic boy I've ever met," I had overheard her say. But I didn't give up, and she didn't give up. In October, when planning a drama trip to New York City, she asked, "What about you, Okey?" In a class of 20 students, it would have been so easy to pretend that an unpromising actor did not exist. Instead, she said again, "What about you, Okey?" "I'll see," I said.

The transformation of "the most undramatic boy" had begun. I acted in every play Mrs. "F" directed during my college years. I made a place for myself socially and artistically in college, and I started down a path that would lead to a life in theater, writing, and education. Today, when I think about everything that is wonderful and magical about the theater and education, I think of Claire Wickersham Fiorentino, Mrs. "F." *What about you?* became the question, the anchor and the wings of my teaching.

What about you, Billy, around whom a circle of light formed as you, dying, called upon God in Edward Albee's *The Zoo Story*? Becky and John? Tall, fragile, funny Becky as Emily, and 6-foot 7-inch, childlike, championship basketball player John, who, together, so touched the audience in Wilder's *Our Town* that the action had to be held until audience sobs began to subside. Steven? Tough, intense, brilliant Steven, who stood at attention in the noonday sun at Annapolis, saying lines in his head from poems that he had learned in class and speeches from Ionesco's *Rhinoceros*. Jimmy? Tall, skinny Jimmy who learned to read while prompting Shaw's *Bury the Dead* and received standing applause from the entire cast when they suddenly realized what had happened.

Nearly a half century ago, a stocky, blue-eyed California boy put his muscular arm around my substantial young shoulders. He had just asked me how to spell "hair." But on seeing that I had opened a book in front of my face to hide the fact that I was sobbing because I was leaving California and would no longer be teaching his class, he said, "Mr. Chenoweth, if you're gonna continue being a teacher, you will have to learn to control your emotions better than that!" Stevie? Jane? Mary Ellen? Becky? Gabe? Sean? Paul? Bruce? And all the casts of all the plays we did together. Thank you for acting your hearts out. I hope that life will be kind and generous to you. I love you.

Every year when I return to school I hope to enter, as I believe my students do, with open arms, an open heart, and an open mind. Even though I have gone to the ends of the earth to learn my art and craft, I shall start a little as I did that long-ago September morning in West Virginia. The new truths of the heart and soul that we discover will be the most surprising ones. The old truths are always there and will make us feel very comfortable and even a little daring as we search for new ones.

In October the huge maple tree outside our window across the parking lot will become the color of apples, grapes, and lemons. I love today because only in this present instant am I truly alive. But I am also looking forward again to October. In October the frost will come and stiffen the grass of the suburban lawns. In the afternoons and evenings, students will come in from the athletic fields and start to work on a major play for the spring. That work will be as good as working life gets.

Shall we take on *Hamlet* this year? We have the talent. Do we have the desire?

What do you think, Chip, Jon, Gary, Marty, Andy, Eve, John, Billy, Mike, Becky, Jerry, Gerard, Elise, Kyle?

In December, when we are hard at work on our chosen play, the snow will begin to fly outside our wall of windows and pile up on the rows of cars in the parking lot. The limbs of our gigantic maple tree will be bare. The iron stove is long gone, but inside, as we work, our hearts will always be spring.

A List of Prayers & a Gift

Okey Canfield Chenoweth

Let me pick up after myself.
Let me say thank you for singing me to sleep.
Let me respond happily to all gifts.
Let me do well in school.
Let me say goodbye gently.
Let me say hello more.
Let me leave behind without abandoning.
Let me repair broken promises.
Let me fulfill expectations.
Let me put your heart back together.
Let me give you back your lost sleep.
Let me separate only when you are ready.
You whom I have torn apart
Let me put back together.
Let me add up all of my grudges and come to zero.
Let me give you everything I kept from you.
Let me make the most of you;
Forgive me for not having done so.
I, hereby, give you all I meant to do.

A Poem for a Child

Okey Canfield Chenoweth

What should go into a poem
for a child?

Should it be an elephant,
or something wild?

Should it be a great long-
necked giraffe?

Or something that laughs and
laughs and laughs?

To find just exactly the
right thing

ALL over the world, I'd go
traipsing.

But if the poem were not for you,
but me,

I'd put in the little girl . . . little boy . . .
right in front of me.

For Winter

Okey Canfield Chenoweth

The dogwood
has withdrawn
its delicate flower

and grown
something hard
for winter.

I, too, am
prepared for
the months ahead.

Brooks

Okey Canfield Chenoweth

Brooks do not laugh.
They speak
of life and death
Marriage and the elements.
Also, they speak of the wind and stars.
And sometimes they speak of children
Who come to bathe their feet
And look for miracles.

Not a miracle man

Okey Canfield Chenoweth

I am not a miracle man.
I do not increase the number of fishes.

And water has remained
water in my hand.
I am not a miracle man.

But I will water any flower
that wants to open,
And in climbing, (try to) give
any climber a hand.

Teacher/mentors

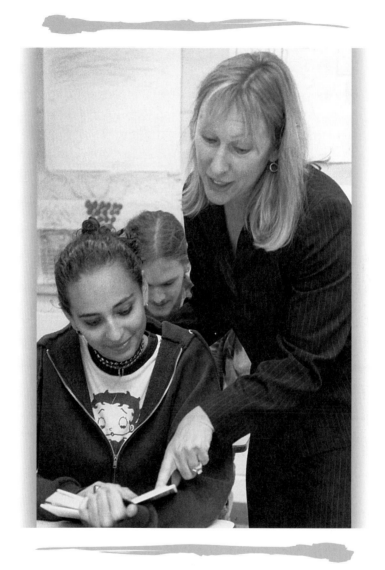

Suzanne H. Snyder-Carroll
7th–12th Grade English Teacher
Hopewell Valley Central High School
Pennington, New Jersey
21 years

It's All About Remembering

Suzanne H. Snyder-Carroll

MR. MURPHY SAT ON THE BROAD windowsill facing the classroom door. He was leaning back, resting, watching the clouds beyond the city skyline, smoking a cigarette. The classroom was dark, mysterious, inviting in a strange way. It was 1966, my sophomore year in high school, and I had never met anyone quite like my new English teacher.

He rubbed his cigarette out on the windowsill, jumped from the sill to the floor in a flash saying, "And God said, 'Let there be light!'" He flicked on the lights hollering, "And don't you dare tell the nuns I smoke!" I didn't know whether to laugh or run. Of course, eventually, it became quite evident that the nuns ignored Mr. Murphy's smoking because he was such a great teacher. His habit of starting class in the dark and then quoting the Bible to dramatize the creation of light became a metaphor for our learning. Each day new lights were going on for us in the world of literature and language. Mr. Murphy was fun, our class was fun, reading was fun because it led to exciting times that began in the dark and evolved into wonderful and unpredictable experiences. For the first time I felt the desire to become a teacher. I wanted to teach others like Mr. Murphy was teaching me: with creativity, with consistency, with energy, with spirit!

Now, over 30 years later, I have been teaching English for 21 years. I can't count the number of times I have reflected on the days I spent in Mr. Murphy's classroom and in those of many other teachers who had their own unique ways of helping me to learn. My memories of those days have sustained me in the desperate moments when I'm driving to school and I feel like turning around, when I'm working on a lesson plan and everything

I come up with seems mundane and boring, when I'm tired and I'm staring at a stack of 72 essays that have to be graded. I conjure up the spirits and the strength of my former teachers when I'm on the verge of thinking, "What for?" and I'm afraid the voice in my head won't have a good answer.

I stop. I go back in my memory to the times when I was trying to learn something and someone had to help me. I go back to the teachers who stood before me or sat down next to me, who put a gentle hand on my shoulder and talked quietly and sincerely to me about how to do something, about ways of thinking, about why certain things work the way they do. I think about teachers who took the time to read my essays, how boring it must have been for them, and how when I was a student I never even thought about my teachers being bored. I remember that many teachers passed through my life, touched my life, changed my life. I never had a chance, or never took the time, to thank them.

I tell myself that today is the day I thank them. Today is the day I pay tribute to them. This day at school will be my best day because it will be taught for them. This lesson plan will come alive because it will be inspired by them. These essays will get my full attention because one day long ago they gave my work their full attention. It is not always about saying thank you; sometimes years and distance and death prevent that. It is about being thankful and doing to the best of my ability what I was taught to do. It is about passing on what was given to me. It is all about remembering that I was once young, immature, and in need of a great teacher. It is all about remembering that it is no accident I was called to this kind of service. I chose it. And now there are young students sitting in my classroom very much in need of a great teacher. I tell myself that I have a responsibility to try to be that great teacher. I tell myself that I have an honorable tradition to uphold and that I am part of an unending cycle much larger than myself. I tell myself that Mr. Murphy and my former teachers are watching me, and smiling.

Carter Jason Sio
9th–12th Grade Woodworking Teacher
Director of Woodworking and Design
George School
Newtown, Pennsylvania
15 years

Shop Thoughts

Carter Jason Sio

I HAVE THE UNIQUE OPPORTUNITY TO teach the art form that I love and practice, the art of furniture making. I teach high school students to build things of beauty out of wood. It is "high school shop" to many, but to me it is so much more. It seems by accident that I became a teacher 15 years ago. However, as I look back on the progression of events that led up to my current teaching job, it is as though I had been in training for it all along.

I grew up around teachers. My uncle and aunt were teachers in Chicago's inner city. My father was a college professor at Colgate University in upstate New York. As a child I was aware that students were visiting our house, sitting in the living room and talking with my dad, staying for dinner. He and my mother were always excited when a former student would stop by, and they took great pride in their students' accomplishments, in and out of the university setting.

I, too, have had some outstanding teachers. One in particular influenced the direction my life would take. My high school woodworking teacher, Palmer Sharpless, a 38-year veteran of teaching, kept in touch with me after I graduated. He always knew what I was doing and where I was living. So when he announced his retirement and placed my name at the top of the list of his possible replacements, word got to me quickly. Although still involved in furniture design and construction, I had my sights set on a more corporate future. Yet the minute I set foot in my old shop on the day of my interview, I knew things were about to change. I haven't looked back since that cold winter day in January.

In many of today's high schools young people are being taught creativity using the computer. There is really very little taught that resembles the crafts of yesterday: Pottery, painting and drawing, woodworking, and metalworking are as foreign to today's students as a rotary phone. Knowing that these crafts are being taught to fewer and fewer young people each year, I approach my teaching with a fervor. This may be the only time they will have the opportunity to work in wood, but if I make the experience unforgettable and enjoyable, maybe the craft will live on through them.

Each student will learn the new skills of sawing, planing, chiseling, and fitting joints differently. Some will marvel at the tactility of the process; others will dream of a time in their future when they own a credit card and can order their furniture from a catalog. But all will have had the experience of making furniture. To take the rough drawing of a concept that originated in one's own head and turn it into a finished product—well, I'm not sure there is any feeling quite like that. I want all my students to experience that feeling. They will have heard the song a sharp plane makes as it slides along the length of a board. They will experience the tedium of fitting a hand-cut joint, and they will marvel at the final product.

I tell my students that they are building the heirlooms of their future, that the work they produce will be handed down through generations, treated with reverence, talked about with pride. As that furniture passes through the hands of family members, as their fingers trace its crisp edges and soft flats, it is also the hand of the teacher living within that carries on—the hand that steadied the dovetail saw, the informed eye making adjustments in a drawing, and the encouraging voice that said, "Keep trying to do your best. This piece will be beautiful when it is done."

Students of mine have gone on to pursue careers in furniture building, architecture, and design. Some are quite accomplished. They visit and call. Sometimes they write. Recently, one of my former students introduced me to a friend as his mentor. "Was I?" I thought to myself. Suddenly, I knew how my father felt when his former students would visit him, and I began to see that after 15 years of teaching, I, too, had an impact on peoples' lives.

Last week, Palmer stopped by to visit and use some shop space. As we were speaking, one of my students quietly interrupted us with a question about her current project, a folding room screen. When I finished speaking with her I turned back to finish our conversation. Palmer was looking at me with a deep, knowing look. A smile spread across his face, and in the voice I've known since I was 16, he said, "Do you know how lucky you are?"

"I do," I replied. "But it sure feels good to hear you say it."

Carter H. Harrison, Jr.
8th Grade English Teacher
Dedham Country Day School
Dedham, Massachusetts
16 years

Snake Skin

Carter H. Harrison, Jr.

JON HAD JOGGED A LITTLE OVER TWO miles and didn't feel like making his run much longer. A left at the fork around the bend would take him back to camp the shortest and easiest way. Summer was almost over. One lowland maple held in its highest branches an open hand of red leaves. Soon Jon would slip into the other routine he knew so well, and at this time of the year he had to admit that he looked forward to it. Some would say that he moved from one chaos into another—director of a summer camp to science teacher in an elementary school. But he found one to complement the other. During the school year he often discovered activities he wanted to try during the summer; during the summer, he learned new ways to present his discipline at school. Each year he found the different routines of his life to be growing more and more alike. At the fork, he decided to take a right.

This direction meant an extra mile, which wasn't so bad except the sun was strong and the route was steep. Jon hadn't run all week. Closing camp required careful supervision for two reasons. The first was obvious. The hot August afternoon made it difficult to imagine the threat of snow, freezing temperatures, and animals seeking shelter. The second was less obvious. He needed to tend to his staff's disappointment. Many of them teachers, they found a deep devotion to their profession during their summers at camp. Jon wanted to make the summer as meaningful for his staff as it was for the children, believing a strong experience for the staff made for a stronger experience for the children. But the children were the heart of the experience, and with them gone home, camp had lost its spirit. To the staff, closing sometimes brought on the winterization of feelings, something Jon believed counterproductive to what he hoped his staff learned over the summer: the importance of sharing what one knows in a way that allows for discovery.

Jon's mind then jumped to the upcoming school year. Amidst all of the routine, there was always something new about September. Once the students entered his class on that first day of school, he felt as though anything could happen; it wasn't so much a feeling of control as it was a feeling of being pulled along—like catching a wave. His desire to share education rather than to give it led him to become a camp director. He hoped that someday he could start his own camp that would provide even broader educational experiences for children—not just experiences based on natural history. Maybe someday the camp wouldn't be restricted only to summer. Maybe someday it could replace the current concept of school.

The hill was steep. The incline focused his attention on the ground, a discouraging focal point for a runner. He felt as though he could walk up with less effort and still go as fast. And then, just to the side of the road, just on the edge of his narrowing field of vision, lying in front of a large, bare, sun-warmed stone he saw it. But he continued running up the hill. The object triggered a synapse long dormant. Brief flashes of images and thoughts interrupted his concentration. He felt as though he had just found something he had been searching for a long time. And he thought of Okie, someone he hadn't thought of in many years.

Waverly was a crowded town, and there Okie lived on a busy street. Okie's house and the barn behind it were a suburban anachronism. The barn, larger than the house it purported to serve, sat squat on enough land to support a gravel drive, neatly edged with a garden and some submissive green grass. As a dinosaur's size reels most imaginations, this placid barn was evidence of a time before shopping malls, a time when developed land meant that it could be farmed: thousands and thousands of acres—not just land, but nature. Sadly, Okie's barn was a time machine, though happily it served its purpose. Behind it a few acres of trapped and condemned second-growth forest hopelessly defended against encroachment.

A few years from retirement, Mr. O'Connell was the only teacher who could be addressed by his nickname, and everyone did. For the younger students who would only see Okie once or twice a week, Okie was reason not to get sick. His visits to their classrooms were visits from the real world of things that crawl under rocks, light that made rainbows, and wind that supported kites. For the older students who were able to visit him more often in the science laboratory, school had become a chore, although science was fun because "you can do things while you're learning."

As an elementary school student who eventually would grow to immerse himself in the sciences, Jonnie Burns did not respond well to his teachers. He liked telling stories. When he was called upon, Jonnie's desire to make people laugh frequently led to his dismissal from class. What he learned in the hall was that learning was not for him. He learned not to try hard in school, and though he didn't fail any subjects, he never did very well in any either—until science his 5th grade year.

During the summer before 5th grade, Jonnie attended "Okie's Camp," a summer program that began and ended each weekday in Okie's barn. What happened between 9:00 a.m. and 4:00 p.m. was the orchestration of young interest under the baton of one of the world's most interesting general know-it-alls and talented storytellers. Jonnie didn't notice that he did very well in science the following year.

The size of Okie's Camp was limited to the number of children who could fit in Okie's station wagon. In the days before seat belts, that number was about 10. Okie took his children to search tide pools, see nesting colonies of shorebirds, visit beekeepers, beach comb, prowl woods and fields, to realize nature that may not be in their backyards—but it was close.

It was in Okie's barn that the children manufactured and warehoused their projects until Okie's Fair at the end of the summer. Terraria, ant farms, birdhouses, and arts and crafts were typical projects. Children always had an ongoing project, and it could be almost whatever they wanted it to be. When the summer began, Jonnie didn't know what he wanted to do, so Okie showed him how to weave a basket. Okie told him, "While you're weaving this, think about something you'd really like to do, and I'll see if I can get you started." If there was anything Okie could do, it was get someone started. Jonnie discovered that he liked basket-weaving and decided to make the largest basket that had ever been made. Then one rainy day, Okie showed the children something that captivated Jonnie, a snake skin that Okie had recently found. He said, as many teachers have said before him, "Just as you grow out of your clothes, snakes grow out of theirs." Jonnie went up to him and asked eagerly, "Where'd you get that?"

"It was in the woods behind the barn," Okie replied sensing interest.

"I want one. I want to find one. I want that to be my next project, to find a snake skin." Jonnie sounded very determined. And Okie liked determination.

"They're not easy to find. You usually find them only when you're not looking for them."

"Please?" Jonnie asked.

Okie liked determination.

Okie convinced Jonnie that there were other interesting things besides just snake skins to be found in the woods behind the barn, and maybe he could look for them as well as snake skins and prepare a small presentation for the fair. Jonnie liked the idea, but he didn't want to make a display as most people did for the fair; he wanted to *talk* about what he found. Okie told Jonnie to go ahead. And then Jonnie added, "If I find a snake skin, I can keep it, right?"

Jonnie didn't find the snake skin that he wanted, but of the many things he discovered in the woods, some of them, he thought, were almost as good as a snake skin. Among them, his favorites were a beetle casing, which Okie explained was like a skeleton, except it was on the outside. Jonnie also found an owl pellet. The owl pellet even surprised Okie.

On the day of the fair, Jonnie was a little upset. It didn't take Okie long to discover that Jonnie was discouraged that the summer was almost over and he hadn't yet found a snake skin. Okie reminded him that snake skins were hard to find. Then he said, "You found an owl pellet: I've never found one in those woods. And just because the fair is tonight doesn't mean you can't continue looking tomorrow for snake skins, and all the other neat things you can find. You can bring them to me at school, and we'll talk about them."

Jonnie was still discouraged, "But I wanted to show a snake skin with my beetle and my owl pellet tonight."

"I'll let you show mine if you're careful with it." Then Okie added, "But I want it back."

Jon Burns had only run about six or seven paces when he realized, "Snake skin! I've been wanting one of those since Okie showed me his." He remembered holding it during the short presentation he gave at Okie's Fair, "The Things You Can Find in Okie's Woods." Young Jonnie treated that skin with reverence. Since that time he had been on many walks—first looking for snake skins, then looking to find the many things he had found when looking for snake skins, then just looking. He had never found a snake skin before, and somehow he thought that finding one no longer mattered. Now that he had found one, he realized that finding one hadn't really stopped mattering; he'd just forgotten that it mattered. Then he thought of other things he had found that had mattered. So much of what made them matter, he realized, was that he had found them himself.

He stopped running. Dripping sweat and breathing deeply, he turned around to search for the brittle skin that lay before that stone. It was only a few strides back. He thought of the good story the skin could illustrate, "This is the first snake skin I ever found. I began looking for it as part of my first science project, but the skin took me over 30 years to find!" Jon had always given a great deal of credit to a science teacher he had in high school and then to some of his professors in college and graduate school. He felt that they had played a significant role in his education. And they had. But he'd never realized how much he had been inspired by Okie before that moment.

He went back to look in front of that bare stone, but what he found was not a snake skin. He found a two-foot long strip of decaying bark. It was broken in several places allowing the strip to be twisted in an "s" shape. There was a moment of disappointment, but he didn't think again of Jonnie-before-the-fair. He allowed himself, this time, to be amused. "I guess I'll just have to keep looking." He smiled and continued his run up the hill; the search for snake skins resumed.

David Downing
2nd Grade Teacher
Belmont Day School
Belmont, Massachusetts
20 years

Window

David Downing

I DO NOT HAVE TO LOOK AT THE CLASS-room clock to know recess is almost over. Jeremy's face is peering in the window of the playground door. He cannot see me because the early June sunshine through the windows is bright, and I have the lights off in the classroom. Jeremy has on his post-recess scowl. When I let the children in he will tell me this morning's list of transgressions against him. I keep quiet for now. If he sees me, he will start knocking on the window to give me a sneak preview. If it were October, I would get up from my desk and dutifully listen to him. But I am tired and cannot think straight. One minute I want to be away from here, at my summer job. The next, I regret that the children and I will be parting ways soon.

At this time of year when a child reads to me, I am listening to him speak in my ear and hearing his voice from the fall in my mind. In September he could not read many of these words. He only read to me at all because I required it. This is progress I could not have predicted, even after teaching for over 20 years. I still teach because of stories like this. Not because a child gained noticeable confidence and proficiency. It is the unpredictability. I never know from one day, one year, to the next what my time in the classroom will be like. Because anything can, and will, happen, I enjoy the time in this room with the same people for a year.

I believe most children have an ability to do a lot of learning on their own (granted, after hours of teacher time creating the right learning environment and teaching students the necessary skills). I do enjoy stand-ing in front of the class explaining a new concept. But I get as much of a boost watching and helping children work on their own. My job is to help them become independent learners. I know that is where I want them to be 20 years from now.

The children have helped me continue to learn, as well. As often as I can I go to Montana to dig for dinosaur bones, a passion that grew from teaching kindergarten children more than 10 years ago. I learn alongside the children. Out of a class discussion last month on how civil war has decimated the gorillas' habitat blossomed the children's curiosity about the Hutu and Tutsi in Rwanda. My ignorance was revealed and inquisitiveness piqued. So off to the library I went. The children's questions about rabies during a study of bats made me again lead them, and me, to the library to study the disease.

The school where I teach is one of many that describes itself as a community of learners. Most of the year I focus on the "learners" part. In June I am wistful about "community." People work hard together in this classroom, whether they are 8 or 45. It makes a strong bond between us. The variety and unpredictability of human emotions, learning styles, and lifestyles creates an interesting and challenging workplace here. When I hear friends tell stories about their own workplaces, where people some-times are not as mature or hardworking as my 8-year-old coworkers, I am glad I work where I do.

I get up and open the playground door: "Jeremy, I have a problem."

He pauses, caught off guard: "You do?"

"Yes. I need a chair for the 3rd grade teacher. She is coming down to talk with all of you. Would you go next door and get one? And I'll listen to what you want to say to me later."

"OK."

I am hoping time will heal some of his social wounds before we talk this afternoon.

I sit at my desk as the 3rd grade teacher tells the class what next year will be like. They listen with rapt attention, and I am a little hurt because they are ready to leave. On the last day of school I will ask the children to write to me this summer. Most won't. I will say hello to them in the hall next year as we pass each other. Most will look at me as if the bulletin board display next to them called out their names. But this is as it should be. A teacher helps students move on. A good teacher makes himself obsolete.

After Words

Kit Frost
Photographer
9th–12th Grade Art Teacher
Bayonne High School
Bayonne, New Jersey
22 years

An Honor to Witness

Kit Frost

THIS BOOK IS REALLY ABOUT PASSIONate *lives*. All of these teachers lead lives filled with imaginative daring, commitment, love, and learning. I am honored to have been chosen to visit with and witness this passion. I am honored because I saw examples of some of the best teaching around; I am honored to have participated in a project designed to celebrate the profession. To experience firsthand, to witness, and to make images that celebrate and validate teaching are what defined my journey.

Crafting portraits of these teachers was a highly individualized undertaking. However, as I traveled around the country visiting the classrooms, homes, and studios of the educators chosen for this book, I noticed certain patterns. Experienced teachers have some things in common. And though this book exemplifies the work of a select group of teachers, it in fact validates and honors the work of *all* teachers. Whether our experience derives from a large urban high school in New Jersey, as mine does, or variously from a small private middle school in California, Louisiana, or Texas—whether the curriculum is taught in Chinese, French, English, or any of an increasingly large number of languages—we can all identify with the moments of love, wonder, surprise, intimacy, struggle, and transition.

My honor to witness included moments of love as expressed in the schoolyard of the International School in Washington, D.C. There, one of Robin Beach's young students hugged her and sat on her lap while she explained the "shell game" in French. When Suzanne Snyder-Carroll's teenagers giggled and played with her while she corrected their English essays, her laughter and love for her students was contagious. And it was my honor to witness when, because it was the last days of the school term and she was leaving to head a new school, Sarah Levine's children spontaneously hugged her and then went off to their classes.

I witnessed a love of and wonder about art in the noise and activity in Douglas DePice's classroom. To call him an art teacher does not do justice to this Renaissance man. Doug's teaching transverses the curriculum, combining art, nature studies, math, and science. I watched and phtographed Margaret Wong as she danced around her classroom to explain enunciation in the Chinese language. Students in Lanie Higgins's science class were excited to be called upon to explain the concepts of force and gravity learned on rides at the school carnival prior to the lesson. And I was impressed when Lucienne Bond Simon blew bubbles in class to amplify her explanation of light and the color spectrum. Even more striking was the way her students' eyes lit up as they understood the concepts she was demonstrating.

I witnessed moments of transition: teacher to administrator, active teaching to retirement, being on sabbatical, returning after a leave of absence. Issues of transition were present for those facing the challenges of 15, 20, or 30 years of teaching and wondering what else lies beyond the classroom. I witnessed the pulls in teachers' lives, challenged to do their best while faced with family demands and personal struggles.

There were great moments of surprise for me, such as when Hamilton Salsich's 8th graders rose to welcome me when I arrived. Indeed I felt surrounded by the "leaders of the future" as I sat in one of his creative writing classes, witnessing the admiration, respect, and collaboration expressed among his students. I will never forget being asked to sit in the "chair of honor" while Lucienne Bond Simon's "backyard friends" sang songs to me.

There were moments of intimacy when I was blessed with the time to get to know some of the teachers beyond the classroom. Okey

Chenoweth recited his poems to me; Louise Wigglesworth read *Ophelia* aloud in her living room. I spent an afternoon at the Opryland Hotel with Vickie Gill where we talked about our common struggle for balance in our multifaceted lives.

All of the teachers in this book are striving to balance their passion for teaching with their love for and need to create. In one of her poems, Adrienne Rich writes: ". . . the more I love my life, the more I love you." Passionate lives are fulfilling lives. They are lives filled variously with writing, painting, dancing—efforts at making their art and their teaching complementary.

Most of all, my journey to take the photographs for this book has been a celebration of individuals who are succeeding in finding balance. They are so passionate about their lives that they do all they can to stay fresh each day in class and to manage their drives to teach, to learn, and to create. The teachers in this book—and the many, many other passionate teachers—love their students and their jobs; they are excited about teaching and excited about their students' and their own learning. All of this and more have been an honor to witness.

Scott McVay

Scott McVay served as the first Executive Director of the Geraldine R. Dodge Foundation
(1976-1998). Throughout that time, and before and since, his life companion
of 40 plus years, Hella—a teacher and learner par excellence—has been a source of strength,
inspiration, and continuity. They are shown here at the 1998 Dodge Poetry Festival.

After Words

Scott McVay

Who will write "You Are My Sunshine?"
Who will lift your spirits when you're low?
Who will make sure your coffee mug fits your finger just so?

Where to begin? Why not at the very beginning? One of the absolute joys of this project is seeing what you find in the net when you are seining for fish—be it a weakfish, a striper, an oyster catcher, a fluke, or a bluefish.

Since I'm tall, I go deep at low tide with a paddle affixed to a long net. It's as though Sarah Levine is the one who pulls her oar closer to shore. We feel a strike, see corks bob; can we bring it in? And there in the net of our continental sweep is the "Dear Governor Foster" pamphlet written at a time when the Louisiana State Legislature was proposing—again—that all state funding for the arts be eliminated. The beguiling text by Lucienne Bond Simon and the pictures by her 2nd graders prompted the Governor to write a thank-you letter to each child and to Mrs. Simon. Funding for the arts was restored *in full* and, subsequently, *increased*.

Throughout the country, we see arts budgets slashed without feeling. As an artist and veteran teacher, she testifies to the transformational power of the arts and a passion for teaching "that offers real hope and substance to education."

All the contributions in the book are from teachers who are essentially artists in evoking the capacities of their students through learning.

THWACK! In a summer when men are vying to surpass Roger Maris's single season record of 61 home runs, Dianne Close—swinging a solid wooden bat with the bases loaded—hits a homerun, to the far bleachers, for number 75. In "Play by Play," Close gives the unblinking reader a sense of the give-and-take in any active classroom where the teacher challenges and is challenged—ceaselessly. The immediacy, the wit, the interplay, tell us a volume, an encyclopedia, about the eternal exchange between the master and numberless apprentices.

What is more authentic than a teacher in action, observing what is really going on, and who, through an experience recollected, distilled in a poem, can catch an essence traveling beyond words. Peter Murphy of Atlantic City High School has written "Still Life with Mothers," which puts you into an hour in his life that will live with you as long as you draw breath. It is no surprise that this poet-teacher has inspired original work in his students, two of whom became Presidential Scholars in the Arts.

Wherever this book falls open, your eye rests on the poignant thought of a seasoned, sensitive teacher. Kristie Wolferman was asked one year to note her "special needs" students. It began to dawn on her that each of her 36 6th graders had "special needs." As she completed the task, she saw, ". . .the last student couldn't be left out because I realized that I had neglected her as soon as I saw her name standing alone as someone with no special needs. She was so perfect that she had never received extra attention, and that needed to be remedied. Perhaps she took her work too seriously. Did she ever have any fun? Now I was worried about the one student I didn't think had any problems at all."

Benj Thomas is attuned to and aware of the times when "somebody is learning something," including, for example, "All of the times that we were all laughing." Ah, yes, laughing is often linked to learning.

With wonderfully crisp, sharp, evocative, inviting writing, Elizabeth June Wells draws us in: "I love chasing words. They writhe and wriggle and defy me to pin them down on the page. And when I think I have won and can afford to collapse in bed, I wake up to discover that in the night those words have crawled off and left only my sweat smeared on the page." She makes stunningly clear what we knew intuitively: "In struggling with language, we create ourselves and our world. As long as my students and I keep language alive and honest, teaching will be worth the struggle."

At the 20-year-mark for the Dodge Foundation in 1995, I invited Harry Wilson to paint two shelves of books that had changed the landscape of our perception. We thought a lot about which books to depict, and several authors met with us (Susan Brownmiller, Amory Lovens, Ralph Nader) to describe the genesis and unfolding of their explorations. What a joy to find a kindred soul in Hamilton Salsich who wanted to be a teacher to help others feel the transforming power of books.

Having personally known master woodworker George Nakashima, author of *The Soul of a Tree* and maker of exquisite furniture of lasting beauty, I was happy to see Carter Sio's essay "Shop Thoughts" wherein he voices pleasures in teaching high school students "to build things of beauty out of wood."

How arresting to read Margaret Wong's opening thought: "I remember an August evening in Nanjing in 1949, the close of a perfectly ordinary day. . . . Although we were about to lose everything, all our money and material property, even our very country, the one thing that no one would ever be able to take from us was the knowledge in our heads." Which led to the choice of teaching as a career (thank heavens!), the teaching of Chinese which has flowered in her students who have become scholars, agents of enlightenment, practitioners of business or law, health care professionals and "even entertainers." Think of the influence of a single great teacher.

So, too, with Wei-ling Wu, a former principal in Shanghai, who in seeing hundreds of her students in the United States "singing, dancing, and speaking Chinese" feels that the little fire in her heart lit by her own teacher years ago "has become an inferno." How blessed we are by her scholarship, her leadership, and her passion for teaching.

Teaching is hard work. It's exhilarating. It's exhausting. It's all-consuming. I know because my wife of 40 years, Hella, taught mathematics and chaired a K–12 department for 25 of those years. Her spirit and example inspired much of what we have sought to do to honor and support good teachers at the Dodge Foundation over the years.

Unlike doctoring or lawyering, teaching—the most honorable and oldest of professions—does not have an explicit, agreed-upon set of practices whereby the true professional is known. Yet within a school or community, the remarkable teachers are *known* and their influence on the direction and capacity of youth is beyond reckoning.

Every one of us remembers an admired teacher, or two—or three—who saw some spark within us, provided a nudge or signal of encouragement, saw something inside worth watering, that enabled us to become who we are today.

Often the teacher hardly knows of the influence or impact until years later, if then, but that influence or impact is an unspoken part of the calling—and precisely why this book is important. A shortage of teachers may or may not occur here or there, but we know that a shortage of great teachers is an ever-present problem for a society whose democracy, vitality, and well being depend utterly on an informed citizenry.

The resonance of the arts to all learning is now part of the literature and common belief even as art and music—among the heralded expressions of the human spirit—are missing or wrenched from the curriculum. At the Dodge Foundation we have undertaken initiatives in poetry and theater that engaged teachers deeply, beginning in 1986 and 1987. In 1992, we sought to back outstanding teachers in the nonverbal arts, the visual arts. Some 78 artist-educators have been assisted to date with summer projects of their own choosing and with projects of their own design within their schools. Over the seven years, the results for the teachers who now constitute a lively in-touch community, and their students, and often their colleagues, are stunning.

I invited one of the artist-educators, Kit Frost, to photograph the educators in this book. Kit Frost lives in Durango, Colorado, where she has opened a community darkroom and arts studio. She made time to travel across America to capture the images and spirits of fellow master teachers.

Indeed, the faces in this book suggest what is hopeful, liberating, and contributory to the American experience—devoted teachers who are lively learners themselves. We are thrilled to be able to put a face to what those teachers have written or created. Kit's portraits complete the book and her own essay, "An Honor to Witness," gives the reader a sense of her admiration for those compatriots who do not seek the limelight—just the chance to work with youth to encourage the very best within them.

A Dream

I dream of a gathering of all these amazing teachers, the representatives of tens of thousands more who are as observant and articulate, at a lofty place in early summer before dawn to hear music of the Highlands, the songs of warblers and thrushes and small sounds close to the Earth, and the children singing in a chorus before a great symphony orchestra behind an intimate consort, celebrating the lands that give us water, hearing the heartbeat of that land, the valleys, the forests, the meadows, the farmlands, the hawks over the Kittatinnies, the mighty, moving, meandering, majestic Delaware, together with the children, their families, their teachers, the farmers, seeing the sun rise as the prospects grow with a deepening ethos in the children and their communities, an ethic whereby they write the poetry, keep journals of their close-to-the-ground observations, make the art, write and sing the music, do the dances of spring at the first flower, of summer at the dappled vegetables and fruits, of fall at the harvest of every kind of squash, potato, and berry, of winter and the shoring up, yes all cycles and seasons. There, as the big sun is hauled or leaps or sprints or crawls over the horizon, wondrous teachers in this book and from the Highlands will come together for the first time to know the profession we praise above all others, the origin of all the other trades and the new ones—teaching—through music and, continuing the pilgrimage down the mountain, to see the wonders wrought by children on display at a college which reflect "A River of Words" and paint and joy in place, in these high watersheds, the source of good water for us water beings. Then, after drinking this in, we'll repair to a place for lunch where the stories can continue, take a leisurely walk in one of the places we love, and on to dinner to mark the publication of *A Passion for Teaching* and the ancient craft the teachers pursue with grace, finesse, and stamina.

The words, the thoughts, the heartbeats, the images here will cheer on those to come, those thinking of becoming teachers, those with slighter experience, and they will remind parents, principals, and others of what the higher reaches of the profession look like in their immense variability.

About the Authors

Sarah L. Levine

Sarah L. Levine has been a teacher, teacher of teachers, and school head for more than 30 years. She has taught in private and public schools. As Associate Director of the Principals' Center at Harvard and Lecturer in Education, she worked with aspiring and practicing school leaders. She served as head of Belmont Day School, in Belmont, Massachusetts for nine years and is currently head of Polytechnic School, in Pasadena, California. Sarah is author of many articles and the book, *Promoting Adult Growth in Schools.*

Scott McVay

Scott McVay was the executive director of the Geraldine R. Dodge Foundation in New Jersey, with giving for education, the arts, well-being of animals, and public issues. His passions embrace his family, whales and dolphins, poetry, books, travel, and creative philanthropy encouraging a sustainable society. McVay has a fascination for how learning occurs. He is the author of several works including discovery of the Song of the Humpback whale described in *Science* and a film on the rare Arctic Bowhead whale.

Kit Frost

Kit Frost is an Art and Photography teacher. She taught at Bayonne High School in New Jersey for 22 years and is now the Director of Smiley Studios in Durango, Colorado. She is teaching art to teens and adults, and facilitating workshops for southwestern Colorado Native Americans. Kit also travels extensively teaching, on assignment, and as a consultant for schools nationwide, giving digital imaging demonstrations and workshops to help districts jump-start their "computer literacy through art" programs.

Robin Alexandra Beach is Preschool Teacher, French Immersion, at the Washington International School, Washington, D.C.

Robert L. Bibens is K–8th Grade Chaplain at Holland Hall School, Tulsa, Oklahoma.

Okey Canfield Chenoweth is 9th–12th Grade Drama and English Teacher at Glen Rock High School, Glen Rock, New Jersey.

Dianne H. Close is 7th–12th Grade Classics Teacher at The Winsor School, Boston, Massachusetts.

Patricia Hall Curvin is 12th Grade English Teacher and English Chair at Arts High School, Newark, New Jersey.

Douglas DePice is 9th–12th Grade Art Teacher at Secaucus High School, Secaucus, New Jersey.

David Downing is 2nd Grade Teacher at Belmont Day School, Belmont, Massachusetts.

Victoria M. Gill is 9th–12th Grade English, Reading, and Journalism Teacher at Cheatham County High School, Ashland City, Tennessee.

Carter H. Harrison, Jr., is 8th Grade English Teacher at Dedham Country Day School, Dedham, Massachusetts.

Lois Marie Harrod is 9th–12th Grade English Teacher at Voorhees High School, Glen Gardner, New Jersey.

Justine S. Heinrichs is 6th–12th Grade String and Orchestra Director at Holland Hall School, Tulsa, Oklahoma.

Lanie Higgins is 6th Grade Science Teacher at McCall Middle School, Winchester, Massachusetts.

Richard A. Lawson is 3rd and 4th Grade Teacher at Nueva School, Hillsborough, California.

Irene E. McHenry is Teacher of Teachers at William Penn Charter School, Philadelphia, Pennsylvania.

Kathy Marzilli Miraglia is PreK–4th Grade Art Teacher at Friends Academy, North Dartmouth, Massachusetts.

Pamela M. Morgan is 6th–9th Grade Learning Strategist at Renbrook School, West Hartford, Connecticut.

Brenda Morrow is 3rd Grade Teacher at St. Clement's Episcopal Parish School, El Paso, Texas.

Peter E. Murphy is 9th–12th Grade English Teacher at Atlantic City High School, Atlantic City, New Jersey.

Todd R. Nelson is Head of Middle School at North Shore Country Day School, Winnetka, Illinois.

Ronald Newburgh is 9th, 11th, and 12th Grade Physics Teacher at The Rivers School, Weston, Massachusetts.

Katharine L. Philip is 9th–12th Grade Art Teacher at Leonia High School, Leonia, New Jersey.

Kathy Prout is K–8th Grade Teacher and Coordinator of Gifted and Talented Programs at Frank Antonides School, West Long Branch, New Jersey.

Rose Ratteray is 4th–8th Grade Media and Technology Teacher at P.S. 22, Jersey City, New Jersey.

Susanne Rubenstein is 9th–12th Grade English Teacher at Wachusett Regional High School, Holden, Massachusetts.

Hamilton Salsich is Middle School English Teacher at Pine Point School, Stonington, Connecticut.

Fausto Sevila is 6th–8th Grade Art Teacher at Luis Muñoz Marin Middle School, Newark, New Jersey.

Lucienne Bond Simon is 1st–3rd Grade Art Teacher at Hammond Eastside Primary School, Hammond, Louisiana.

Carter Jason Sio is 9th–12th Grade Woodworking Teacher and Director of Woodworking and Design, George School, Newtown, Pennsylvania.

Suzanne H. Snyder-Carroll is 7th–12th Grade English Teacher at Hopewell Valley Central High School, Pennington, New Jersey.

Beth Spencer is 4th Grade Teacher at Roosevelt School, Neenah, Wisconsin.

Bettye T. Spinner is 12th Grade English Teacher at Moorestown High School, Moorestown, New Jersey.

Jane Sprouse is K–8th Grade Learning Specialist at Katherine Delmar Burke School, San Francisco, California.

Benjamin H. Thomas is 9th–12th Grade Social Studies Teacher at Thornton Friends School, Silver Spring, Maryland.

Nette Forné Thomas is 9th–12th Grade Art Teacher and Art Chair at Arts High School, Newark, New Jersey.

Elizabeth June Wells is 9th–12th Grade English Teacher at St. Martin's Episcopal School, Metairie, Louisiana.

Louise Wigglesworth is 9th–12th Grade Drama and Visual Arts Teacher at Pinelands Regional High School, Tuckertown, New Jersey.

Harry E. Wilson, Jr., is K–12th Grade Director of Art Education in the Summit Public Schools, Summit, New Jersey.

Patricia E. Wilson is K–5 Visual Arts Teacher at Harvard-Kent Elementary School, Charlestown, Massachusetts.

Kristie C. Wolferman is 6th Grade Teacher and Language Arts Chair at Pembroke Hill School, Kansas City, Missouri.

Margaret M. Wong is 9th–12th Grade Teacher of Chinese and Director of International Education at Breck School, Minneapolis, Minnesota.

Wei-ling Wu is 9th–12th Grade Teacher of Chinese at West Windsor-Plainsboro High School, Princeton Junction, New Jersey.

ABOUT ASCD

Founded in 1943, the Association for Supervision and Curriculum Development is a non-partisan, nonprofit education association, with international headquarters in Alexandria, Virginia. ASCD's mission statement: *ASCD, a diverse, international community of educators, forging covenants in teaching and learning for the success of all learners.*

Membership in ASCD includes a subscription to the award-winning journal *Educational Leadership*; two newsletters, *Education Update* and *Curriculum Update*; and other products and services. ASCD sponsors affiliate organizations in many states and international locations; participates in collaborations and networks; holds conferences, institutes, and training programs; produces publications in a variety of media; sponsors recognition and awards programs; and provides research information on education issues.

ASCD provides many services to educators—prekindergarten through grade 12— as well as to others in the education community, including parents, school board members, administrators, and university professors and students. For further information, contact ASCD via telephone: 1-800-933-2723 or 703-578-9600; fax: 703-575-5400; or e-mail: member@ascd.org. Or write to ASCD, Information Services, 1703 N. Beauregard St., Alexandria, VA 22311-1714 USA. Find ASCD on the World Wide Web at http://www.ascd.org.

ASCD's Executive Director is Gene R. Carter.

1999–2000 ASCD Executive Council

President: Joanna Choi Kalbus, Lecturer in Education, University of California at Riverside, Redlands, California

President Elect: LeRoy E. Hay, Assistant Superintendent for Instruction, Wallingford Public Schools, Wallingford, Connecticut

Immediate Past President: Thomas J. Budnik, School Improvement Coordinator, Heartland Area Education Agency, Johnston, Iowa

Bettye Bobroff, Executive Director, New Mexico ASCD, Albuquerque, New Mexico

Martha Bruckner, Chair and Associate Professor, Department of Educational Administration and Supervision, University of Nebraska at Omaha, Nebraska

John W. Cooper, Assistant Superintendent for Instruction, Canandaigua City School District, Canandaigua, New York

Michael Dzwiniel, High School Chemistry Teacher, Edmonton Public Schools, Edmonton, Alberta

Sharon A. Lease, Deputy State Superintendent for Public Instruction, Oklahoma State Department of Education, Oklahoma City, Oklahoma

Leon Levesque, Superintendent, Lewiston School District, Lewiston, Maine

Francine Mayfield, Director, Elementary SchoolBased Special Education Programs, Seigle Diagnostic Center, Las Vegas, Nevada

Andrew Tolbert, Assistant Superintendent, Pine Bluff School District, Pine Bluff, Arkansas

Robert L. Watson, High School Principal, Spearfish 402, Spearfish, South Dakota

Sandra K. Wegner, Associate Dean, College of Education, Southwest Missouri State University, Springfield, Missouri

Peyton Williams Jr., Deputy State Superintendent, Georgia State Department of Education, Atlanta, Georgia

Donald B. Young, Professor, Curriculum Research & Development Group, University of Hawaii, Honolulu, Hawaii